PRAIRIE SCHOONER

STORIES, POEMS, ESSAYS, AND REVIEWS SINCE 1926

Glenna Luschei Endowed Editor-in-Chief:
Kwame Dawes

Managing Editor: Ashley Strosnider

Web Editor: Paul Hanson Clark

Designer: Nathan Putens

Copyeditor: Linnea Fredrickson

Assistant Editors—Fiction:
Robert Fuglei, Raul Palma

Assistant Editors—Poetry:
Arden Eli Hill, Rebecca Macijeski

Assistant Editor—Nonfiction:
Sarah Fawn Montgomery

Editorial Assistants: Belinda Acosta, Thomas Bennitt, Kristi Carter,

April Darcy, Ryler Dustin, Katelyn Hemmeke, David Henson, Zach Mueller, Xavier Navarro, Maria Nazos, Katie Pryor, Dillon Rockrohr, Ian Rogers, Katie Schmid, Jeannette Schollaert, Cameron Steele, Nick White, Cory Willard, Ivan Young

Alumni Readers: DeMisty Bellinger, Steven Edwards, Cody Lumpkin, Carrie Shipers, Laura Madeline Wiseman

BOOK PRIZE SERIES

Series Editor: Kwame Dawes
Coordinator: Katie Schmid
Senior Readers: Grace Bauer, Stephen C. Behrendt, Kate Flaherty, Erin Flanagan

Published quarterly: March, June, September, December. Subscriptions: $28 one year; $45 two years; $65 three years; single copies, $9.00 (Nebraska residents add sales tax); for libraries, $30.00 per year. Add $10.00 per year for foreign subscriptions. Special rates for bulk orders.

Prairie Schooner is published in cooperation with the University of Nebraska Press and the Creative Writing Program of the University of Nebraska-Lincoln English Department and is endowed by the Glenna Luschei Endowed Editorship and Fund for Excellence at Prairie Schooner. Members of the faculty of the creative writing program include Jonis Agee, Grace Bauer, Joy Castro, Kwame Dawes, Ted Kooser, Amelia María de la Luz Montes, Timothy Schaffert, and Stacey Waite. *Submission information may be found at the end of the contributor notes.* Business correspondence should be directed to the Managing Editor. Prairie Schooner is a member of the Council of Literary Magazines and Presses, the Council of Editors of Learned Journals, is indexed with Humanities International Complete, Book Review Index, Index of American Periodical Verse, Current Contents, and Humanities Index and is reproduced by National Archive Publishing Company. It is distributed by Ingram Periodicals, LaVergne, TN, Media Solutions, Madison, AL, and Source Interlink, Bonita Springs, FL. Periodicals postage paid at Lincoln and additional mailing offices. *Postmaster:* Send address changes to Prairie Schooner, 123 Andrews Hall, University of Nebraska, Lincoln, NE 68588-0334. ISSN 0032-6682 USPS #441440 *To subscribe*: Call 1-800-715-2387. We accept MasterCard and Visa. The Lawrence Foundation Award ($1,000), the Virginia Faulkner Award for Excellence in Writing ($1,000), the Edward Stanley Award ($1,000), the Glenna Luschei Prairie Schooner Awards (one of $1,500 and ten of $250 each), the Bernice Slote Award ($500), the Prairie Schooner Strousse Award ($500), the Hugh J. Luke Award ($500), and the Jane Geske Award ($250) are awarded annually to the authors of the best work published in Prairie Schooner. *Initial Luschei Editor-in-Chief*: Hilda Raz. Copyright © 2015 University of Nebraska Press. All rights reserved.

http://prairieschooner.unl.edu

Contents

Volume 90, Number 1, Spring 2016

	Awards 5
Laura Elizabeth Woollett	Working Girl, *essay* 9
Marilyn Hacker	Calligraphies II, *poem* 15
Rigoberto González	Adelina, *essay* 21
Achy Obejas	The Maldives, *story* 31
Annie Finch	Letter to Shahid Ali, in a Warm September, *poem* 40
Wendy Barker	Surgery, A Little History, *poem* 43
Margaret Randall	When Justice Felt at Home, *poem* 45
Ron Paul Salutsky	Elegy with a Heart-Shaped Box, *poem* 46
David Crouse	I'm Here, *story* 50
Lynne Knight	A Brief History of Landscape Painting | Forbidden, *poems* 64
Claire Schwartz	for Mrs. Halachmi | distance is the primal fact, *poems* 67
Ephraim Scott Sommers	Impossible Kiss | My Father Sings Dylan at Sixty-Two, *poems* 71
Emily Vizzo	Lucky, *poem* 73
Jay Merill	Breaking Free, *story* 74
Michael Fulop	The Family | My Daughter's Courage | A Summer Storm, *poems* 82
Joannie Stangeland	Poem to Chibok, Nigeria | Prodigal, *poems* 84
Karen Craigo	The Houses We See from the Highway, *poem* 86
Paul Martin	The Radish | Ghost, *poems* 87
Julie Henson	Diplomatic Efforts, Ouija Board | And the Abyss, *poems* 89
Bernard Matambo	In the Name of the Tongue | The Last time I Saw Annamore Tsonga, *poems* 92
Sarah Giragosian	Easter Dinner, *poem* 94
Kerry Cullen	Parts, *story* 95

Nicholas Samaras	The Exiled Child Looks Back, *poem* **108**
Angie Macri	Landlocked | The Alligator Goes No Farther North than This, *poems* **110**
Robert Newman	Morning Coffee, *poem* **112**
Michael Fessler	The Inner-Peace Initiative, *story* **113**
Todd Fredson	Heckling Paradise | Anniversaire | History Offers No Instruction | A Toast, *poem* **133**
Kira Taylor	Turkey Vultures, *poem* **137**
Joseph Bathanti	Emerson Street | The North Game | Haircut, *poems* **138**
Shruti Swamy	Night Garden, *story* **145**
Elise Juska	The English Teacher, *story* **150**
Brian Patrick Heston	The Giants | Apocalypse Detroit, *poems* **170**
Jennifer J. Pruiett-Selby	In Absence | Hemispheres | Under Pretense of Law, *poems* **173**

REVIEWS

Karen Munro	*Gutshot*, Amelia Gray **177**
Jaime Brunton	*The Lost Novel*, James Shea **179**
Catherine Thomas	*The Seven Stages of Anger and Other Stories*, Wendy J. Fox **180**
P. E. Garcia	*The Physics of Sorrow*, Georgi Gospodinov **182**

Contributors and cover credit **184**

THE LAWRENCE
FOUNDATION AWARD
$1000
for the best short story published
in *Prairie Schooner* in 2015
Ezra Olson
for the story "Marco
Polo" in Fall 2015

THE VIRGINIA FAULKNER
AWARD FOR EXCELLENCE
IN WRITING
$1000
for work published in
Prairie Schooner in 2015
Lawrence Lenhart
for the essay "The Well-Stocked
and Gilded Cage: Psittaculture
Nervosa" in Summer 2015

THE EDWARD STANLEY AWARD
$1000
for poetry published in
Prairie Schooner in 2015
Charif Shanahan
for four poems in Summer 2015

THE BERNICE SLOTE AWARD
$500
for the best work by a
beginning writer published
in *Prairie Schooner* 2015
Dima Alzayat
for the story "In the Land
of Kan'an" in Fall 2015

THE ANNUAL PRAIRIE
SCHOONER STROUSSE AWARD
$500
for the best poem or group
of poems published in
Prairie Schooner in 2015
Aracelis Girmay
for four poems in Fall 2015

THE HUGH J. LUKE AWARD
$250
for work published in
Prairie Schooner in 2015
Natalie Diaz
for the essay "A Body of
Athletics" in Winter 2015

THE JANE GESKE AWARD
$250
for work published in
Prairie Schooner in 2015
Sarah Cornwell
for the story "Mr. Legs"
in Spring 2015

GLENNA LUSCHEI *PRAIRIE SCHOONER*
AWARDS FOR WORK PUBLISHED IN
PRAIRIE SCHOONER IN 2015

Laura Van Prooyen
for five poems in Fall 2015
$1500

Martha Collins
for five poems
in Summer 2015
$250

Tyree Daye
for three poems
in Fall 2015
$250

Emily Geminder
for the essay
"Coming To: A Lexicology
of Fainting"
in Summer 2015
$250

Gregory Pardlo
for the essay
"Cartography"
in Fall 2015
$250

Adrienne Celt
for the story
"The Girls They Burned"
in Summer 2015
$250

Matthew Dickman
for the poem
"Can We Have Our Ball Back"
in Winter 2015
$250

Eileen Myles
for the poem
"St. Joseph Father of Wales"
in Winter 2015
$250

Sujata Shekar
for the story
"Throw Away Nothing"
in Fall 2015
$250

Safiya Sinclair
for four poems
in Summer 2015
$250

Aurvi Sharma
for the essay
"Eleven Stories of
Water and Stone"
in Spring 2015
$250

Members of the Department of
English at the University of Nebraska
are not eligible for these prizes.

Prairie Schooner and its editorship are endowed in perpetuity by the Glenna Luschei Fund for Excellence at *Prairie Schooner* at the University of Nebraska Foundation. This endowment provides eleven annual Glenna Luschei *Prairie Schooner* Awards in the amount of $4,000.

Laura Elizabeth Woollett

Working Girl

I want to be a model or a writer. I am neither of these things. What I am is fifteen and five foot eight, with collarbones deep enough to drink my black coffee out of, a head full of dreams, and a job with Western Australia's largest and only Sunday newspaper. The job is my first job. The job is a high-paying job, which earns me four times as much as my friends' jobs and will allow me to buy spaghetti-strap singlets from KOOKAÏ, three-inch stilettos from ZU, a pastel polo with a Hilfiger flag on the breast, a black French Connection t-shirt that alludes to fucking but in a clever and expensive way. It isn't the job of my dreams, but it does let me skip dinner and leaves me smelling of ink.

I tell my mum, when she drops me off, that I will eat at Dad's. I tell my dad that I already ate at Mum's, and then smugly spend the hour while my stepmother gets ready nursing my Nescafé and watching FashionTV and prodding my little sisters' fat until they whine or giggle. My stepmother gets ready loudly. She talks on the phone and calls my dad Mas! and if she sneezes, she makes a heart-stopping sound. At a quarter past five, she jangles into the kitchen with her red lips and Jakarta Vuitton and slaps the pizza money on the counter, and I am already homesick.

"Ready Luluuuuu?" she drawls.

It is still light when we leave the yellow brick house. If it is summer, the light is thirsty and gold; if it is winter, blue and sad like piano music. My stepmother's blue-black hair flashes ahead of me, the vaccine scar on her bare arm, the thin bar of flesh above her low-slung tracky dacks. She is five feet tall and as glamorous as it's possible to be in stretchy gray polyester, like an actress snapped on her way to Starbucks.

Someday, I will live in a city with Starbucks.

The drive is ugly, warrens of pale brick and gas stacks and dam-like expanses of freeway. I clench my stomach to keep it from grumbling too loudly and also because I'm anxious for the drive not to end. It is always better to be going someplace than it is to be in the actual place; I understand this, and that stopping is to be feared the same as death. This is why I sometimes ride the bus after school a few stops too long.

"You remember Jamie?" my stepmother asks me one afternoon, both of us squinting through oversized sunglasses past the windshield's glare. I know the boy she means, or think I do, and my heart skips because he is pretty, so pretty I have no clue how I could've forgotten his existence for so long. It was many months ago that I sat in a dark room with him and watched the Occupational Health and Safety video, and afterward took a test about the video, and covertly took in his beautiful green eyes and chestnut hair and imagined having him as a boyfriend, and never exchanged a word. We were supposed to start work at the same time. There must be an exciting reason for the holdup. I tell my stepmother I remember and matter-of-factly she says, "He died."

"Oh," I say. "Like . . . actually died?"

"Car crash. So sad, lah. He was *cute*."

My stepmother and I don't often talk of deep things, and don't talk as easily as when I was seven. When we do talk, it's of the things money can buy, the songs on the radio, the people at work, my older sister. "Lazyyyy," my stepmother likes to say about my older sister, who is seventeen and mortal in ways I'm not: has a boyfriend and ex-boyfriends, makes average grades, stresses over her exams, has been to parties with alcohol. I'm good at school without trying too hard, work every Saturday night instead of going out, have never kissed a boy. But if I were more like my sister, perhaps I would've spoken to Jamie and made him my boyfriend and perhaps in this alternate universe he wouldn't be dead.

"Yeah," I say. "He was."

We are almost always early to work. I do not like being early because it means standing outside the factory and talking to people, or really standing to the side while my stepmother talks. My stepmother is good at talking. She talks to the coarse-faced Aussie men and women with their crow-like voices, and to the fat boy who goes to my school and drives a forklift, and most of all to the other Indonesian women. I like the Indo women best because their hair is shiny and because I don't have to pretend to be interested when they talk, though there are words I understand: *mas*, husband; *anak*, kid; *tidak papa*, no problem. Sometimes my stepmother paws my arm unexpectedly and my face heats up like a fire just fanned.

"Right, darlinggg?" she purrs, then cackles like a witch.

My stepmother is a wicked stepmother. Her fingernails are long and her laughter scares me. My stepmother is a good witchy mother, who found me a job that pays twenty-five dollars an hour and makes sure I get to it on time and doesn't mind if I don't eat because she doesn't either. She does smoke, menthol cigarettes from a flashy gold packet, as guiltlessly as a goldfish drinks water. I would like to smoke. I have not eaten since Friday night, will not eat again until Sunday afternoon.

There is a canteen attached to the factory that serves brown and yellow food from a bain-marie. This is *bule* food, white people food, and looks as crude and solid to me as actual shit. I am aligned with the Indo women in my contempt for this food, the *bule* who need to stuff their faces with pies and chips to get through five hours of manual labor. I watch them watch the *bule* like a clowder of black-haired cats, listen out for the bitchy words that give me so much pleasure.

"*Aduh! Gendut!*" So fat!

Then they laugh their wicked smoky laughter and I smile, as much as a good girl can smile over wicked things.

My idols are Nietzsche and Mischa Barton. I have not read a whole book by Nietzsche, but I know he is a great philosopher and I like the things he says on Wikiquote: *God is dead. If you gaze long enough into the abyss, the abyss will gaze back into you. One must have chaos in one to give birth to a dancing star.* I have not met Mischa Barton, but I want to wear the greenish-blue Chloé dress she wore on a red carpet, and to have her cute squarish cheekbony face with the cute squarish smile, and to talk in her unlikely fake California accent with the British undertones. I want to be Mischa Barton's alter ego, Marissa from *The O.C.*, who is a pretty rich girl but also very tragic and who says philosophical things like, "I have no one" and "I don't know why I'm here" and "Do you ever wonder what your life looks like through someone else's eyes?"

I wonder about my life too, how it looks and why I am here.

I pee with my stepmother in the tiny, ill-lit factory bathroom, check my unmade face and ponytail. I have read enough to know that beautiful girls are not discovered in the world's most beautiful places but in factories, slums, hopeless zones where their thin wrists and cheekbones look as rare as pearls. I am mindful of this as I say goodbye to my stepmother at the earplug dispenser, take my bristle-less broom from the wall, and bear it sceptre-like to my work station. It is a few minutes to six. On the hour, the machinery above us will grind into motion, set my nerves on edge.

I am a newspaper sweeper. I work in a pair with another newspaper sweeper, always a woman, almost always Indo, to sweep newspapers from under the great rolling machine that spits them out. The machine is not meant to spit newspapers but to assemble them; however, machines are fallible and it's our job as sweepers to make up for this. Sweepers must move swiftly. Sweepers are stronger than they look.

It's usual for my sweeping partner to already be at the work station by the time I arrive. All the Indo women I work with are punctual like my stepmother; I wonder if this is something that just comes with the territory, like shiny hair and making the most of small spaces. We smile at each other, exchange names, and instantly forget them. She goes back to reading her TV guide. I set down my prized fake Burberry backpack, lay out the things that will help me through the evening:

1 x yellow factory-issue earplugs
1 x 600 ml Diet Coke
3 x Mentos, original mint

I look around for something to read.

People say menial work kills the imagination, but the moment the machines start, I feel my mind crossing over to a plane where nothing is real and everything is what I make it.

If the newspapers come in soft falls, I pretend I am raking leaves. Or I pretend I'm a starved street urchin, grubbing around in the gutters. Or else that I'm living in a dystopian society, where everything is noise and Nietzschean abysses. If they come hard and fast, I pretend I'm digging my way out of an avalanche. Or I pretend I'm under siege, and that the broom is my gun. Or else that I'm the victim of a terrorist attack, seeing everything through a chemical haze: scrap metal, shattered glass, the redness of my own blood before blacking out.

Sometimes we cannot keep up with the newspapers and the glass barrier turns white as a bank of snow and the machine jams, and a man in a Hi-Vis vest has to turn off the machine. These are moments like death, absurd and suddenly quiet. We watch the man wade through our chaos, impersonal as a soldier or a police officer, and do the mysterious, irrelevant things that men do in such situations.

"She'll be right," the man says. "Give us a shout when you've cleared 'em and I'll turn her on again."

We are bathed in sweat, trembling in our sneakers, our hands and jawlines smeared black. We nod and say, "Thank you."

I turn sixteen in the summer. I learn the taste of alcopops and kiss a couple of boys, none of them as beautiful as beautiful dead Jamie. Summer turns to autumn, and autumn to winter, and everyone is talking about the little Filipino girl who was raped and murdered in the toilets of the shopping centre near our factory.

"Mate of mine is going out with one of the homicide detectives," one of the Aussie women is saying. "She says it's *way* gorier than the newspapers are saying."

"Like how?"

The outside of the factory is barren and yellow-lit, like a place where people regularly get murdered. Beside me, my stepmother is silent, her red lips a spell, her dragon nostrils taut; she has daughters who are younger and softer than we are.

"Bastard broke all her arms and legs trying to get her clothes off. Crushed her larynx. That's this bone here."

"*Ughh-ahhh*, poor little thing."

"Poor baby."

"Did it all in under five minutes too. Just shows, can't leave 'em alone for a second."

"Well, at least it was quick."

"Five minutes of *that* though."

The sky is completely black. Puffs of smoke move across it like little girl ghosts. I am pale like a moonflower, university-bound, with nothing in my stomach and no one in my heart. Yet there are things that touch me still.

"Sick bastard. Deserves the death penalty."

"My mate says he's a retard." The woman lets out a luxurious funnel of smoke. "Not that that's any excuse."

At the end of my shift, there is too much ink on my body to wash off in the factory bathroom, no matter how much soap I use or how much I scrub. I know that when I get home and pass a Clean & Clear wipe over my face, it will be stained black; that the shower water that swirls between my feet will be dirtier than Indonesian tap water. My stepmother comes out of her cubicle and declares, "*Eee-yuckk*, my boogie black."

I laugh. I too was just picking my nose in the adjacent cubicle, marveling over the unnatural blackness of what came out.

The late-night radio plays crappy club music that doesn't offend my sixteen-year-old ears: Basement Jaxx, DJ Sammy, Armand Van Helden. We crank it up as my stepmother drives me back to my mum's place, in an older and leafier suburb where the houses aren't all neat brick boxes. It's a longer drive than the drive back to Dad's, and a drive that takes her out of her way, but somehow it's implicit that I prefer to sleep in my own bed after these strange nights of manual labor. Tomorrow, I will go shopping with my best friend, who is pretty and not a virgin. We will meet at noon at the city bus shelter and weave in and out of every shop containing objects of beauty, and lift them up, and hold them against us, and try them on in mirrored rooms. In one of these shops, I will buy something divine and wrapped in tissue, and take it home with me on the bus in a shiny bag. At home, I will lay it on my bed and unwrap it in secret like chocolate and inhale its scent and delay removing the tags, and dream and dream of the day when everything in my life is as beautiful as the things money can buy.

Marilyn Hacker

Calligraphies II

Self-referential,
a text that explains itself.
Al-Mutanabbi

known by lance, pen, desert, sword.
My horse and my notebook think

what I am thinking
through an orgy of cadence.
I loved one woman

whose heart gave out when she read
my letter, that I'd return.

*

He could not return:
price on his head, defector.
His mother, with whom

he talked about books on Skype
through bomb-shattered nights in her

once-tranquil suburb,
was going, not back to the
mountains, not Beirut:

road of the insurrection
in her cells. Could not return.

*

Obsessive return
to the site of departure
or abandonment:

checkpoint south of Reyhanli,
a bar in the rue Charlot—

something changed for good.
She got up and walked away.
A guard waved them through.

And the next day and the next
were going to be different.

*

It is different
waking in the city that
used to be your home.

You are what you are knowing
you are not that anymore,

as old as your friend
when he wrote his late pages
sparring with Bashô

while his sorrel-haired muse fixed
his lunch, pining for cities.

*

The question of lunch,
whether a parenthesis
of conversation

in a cheerful public place
(Tah Marbutah, Hamra Street),

exiles and expats
eating maqdous and kibbeh
in three languages,

or standing near the fridge with
labneh, two verbs, and a spoon.

*

At least two verbs for
departure, five for desire,
come swiftly to mind

from her schoolgirl lexicon.
And all the horses, learned when

she was younger, hoped
to ride away on this new
alphabet, across

deserts of habit and waste
through the six-vocabled dawn.

*

Rainy-fingered dawn
prods the grimy scaffolding
outside the window.

Wet slate roofs, blurry slate sky
swell the list of erasures

you count down, waking.
A sea north of the morning,
a wind from elsewhere—

idea of departure, and
an overstayed welcome.

*

She has overstayed
her transit visa more than
six weeks now. She was

refused a work permit, but
she goes daily to her class,

translates as-Sayyab's
rainsong with them to English,
not their first language.

No news from the Ministry
of Labor. War news from home.

*

A long walk home down
the mango-and-sari street,
then the boulevard's

cheap phone cards to Sénégal,
small real estate agents who

upscale old buildings
pricing the immigrants out.
I'd rather live here.

I'd rather live anywhere
than in my worn-out old skin.

*

Under bruise-red skin,
the Pakistani mango's
sweet wet orange flesh,

mix it with labneh in a
blue-purple bowl from Konya—

where your Kurdish friend
said he'd first heard Rumi
in his mother tongue.

All of you sharing treasures
that no one bequeathed to you.

*

He's inherited
another histrionic
refugee. Curses,

silently, his friend, lavish
with others' time and ideas.

Thinks of his uncle's
trek from Lodz to Liverpool
thanks to a letter,

and calls a man who knows a
man in the right ministry.

*

Give the right answer
in the right tone of voice to
the right person who

ate the right thing for lunch and
drank the right dose of caffeine:

you may walk out with
the right papers to claim your
identity card,

your day relentlessly, you
might say, self-referential.

Rigoberto González

Adelina

The summer after we moved in with my grandparents, the idea was born to bring back "una muchacha"—a young woman—from Mexico. The purpose was to find a caretaker for my father, recently widowed, and a nanny for my brother and me, recently orphaned at ages ten and twelve. Abuela, the only female in the small two-bedroom cinderblock apartment, had become exhausted managing a household that had doubled overnight. It seemed like a good solution though I couldn't imagine where they were thinking of housing this seventh body. My grandparents slept in one bedroom, and my father, brother, and my bachelor uncle slept in the other. I slept on the couch in the tiny living room. This didn't bother me much because I had never had my own bed (that wouldn't happen until my freshman year in college), and sleeping in the apartment's most open space gave me the impression I had a room of my own or at the very least a place to breathe, to daydream, and to cry in complete privacy when I remembered my mother. When I couldn't sleep I'd simply pull a chair into the tiny kitchen and read under its dim light, the only light that didn't bother Abuelo, who always kept his bedroom door ajar in order to keep track of our movements. In any case, I didn't dare ask the obvious questions: Where would she sleep? Would I have to give up my couch?

The plan wasn't discussed with me, but I picked up snippets of conversation over time. Since I was a reader, I became invisible behind a book, and somehow my grandparents thought I also became deaf because they would speak frankly in front of me about subjects that would make them hush whenever anyone else walked in.

"She won't be expensive," Abuelo assured Abuela, who nodded in agreement. The long pause that followed made me wonder where their minds had drifted. Perhaps to the convenience of the situation: that a young woman from Mexico would be easy to control, perhaps even easy to take advantage of.

I couldn't imagine what young woman would accept such a position, traveling so far away just to live with a family of farmworkers in a compact unit of southern California housing projects. I had seen a few Mexican films that touched on the subject of poor young women who left their small villages for an opportunity to thrive, but in all cases, they went to live in big-city apartments or suburban homes owned by lawyers, doctors, or businessmen. But in the film narratives, the poor young women didn't have to leave the country. It dawned on me then why this was an especially important detail: the young woman we'd be bringing back would be undocumented, making her even more vulnerable.

Locating a coyote who could smuggle a young woman across was a relatively easy search. We lived a few hours from the border. Over the years reports traveled through the streets about so-and-so's cousin or so-and-so's nephew arriving safely, and the community took note of the coyote's reputation and his contact information to pass along in the most clandestine of referrals. Crossing her over was not the problem. Finding her, that was the sticking point. Or so I thought.

Every summer my grandparents traveled to Michoacán, Abuelo behind the wheel of his truck, annoyed and exasperated after the first day on the road. I had made the trip a few times before so I knew the code of conduct in the camper. Basically, become invisible, inaudible—something I was very good at around Abuelo, who snapped at the smallest things. He held a particular dislike for my brother, who hadn't learned to be silent. Given a choice, Alex would not have joined us on that trip, but he didn't have a choice. Not anymore. As soon as my father moved us into our grandparents' domain we were expected to surrender completely. So there we were the following July, lying down among the piles of secondhand clothing my grandparents took back to their homeland. Whether they sold it or gave it away I never found out.

The two-day drive was utterly boring. The camper didn't have much in terms of windows but in reality there wasn't much to see. When we passed by some little town it looked exactly like the one before with the same buildings and people who wore the same coats and dresses as the citizens of the town just before it. My brother, mad that he had been dragged on this journey, lost himself in sleep since it was too noisy in the back to even hold a conversation. I had withdrawn into a quiet depression after my mother died so I had no problem letting go of any emotion or expectation, though I did feel bad for my brother, who was more active and spirited. The two-day trip in that tomb must have driven him crazy. I tried not to dwell on the helplessness of the situation because I had no power. Neither of us did. This was our new life without our mother: getting sucked into the whims of our very complicated Abuelo.

When we finally made it to Michoacán I was surprised when we stopped in a small mountain village just before Zacapu, my family's hometown. When Abuelo lifted the camper door the light spilled in and the air was invigorating. I knew right away where we had arrived—to El Pueblito, where our distant Purépecha relatives, the cheese-makers, lived. Before we left Zacapu to migrate to California, we made frequent visits here to pick up cheese and to drop off the gallons of spoiled milk. Our El Pueblito relatives were as small and dark as Abuela, they had a peculiar way of shaking hands, and they walked on the mountain paths on bare feet. The village was a series of wooden shacks with chickens pecking about and exposed kitchens where our relatives knelt on the ground over their stone metates to shape the curdled milk into beautiful wheels of cheese. The acidic smell in the air was overwhelming. On weekends the cheese-makers traveled to Zacapu to sell their product at the market or on the plaza, but my city relatives came up by bus for the family discount.

After the initial hand-shaking and samplings of cheese, Abuelo made it clear that my brother and I had to wander about so that the adults could talk. So we did. We kicked at the weeds near the walls made with boulders and pelted rocks at each other. Later I figured out that this was the moment when a young woman had been chosen to make that long journey back to the United States with us. The efficiency of the agreement didn't surprise me, not with Abuelo's temperament. He was an impatient man, and anyone who dealt with him had to move just as quickly, just as impulsively.

We left El Pueblito and showed up, wheels of cheese in hand, at Abuelo's sister's house in the heart of Zacapu. Tía Sara lived in a multiunit complex with a courtyard hidden from street view by a heavy wooden door that was kept bolted shut. I had no idea we'd be back to El Pueblito near the end of our visit to pick up Adelina, a terrified young woman only a few years older than me, so during the next few days, my brother and I walked in and out of Tía Sara's home in ignorant bliss, visiting relatives from our mother's side of the family and making frequent trips to the plaza where we spent our allowance on gelatin cups and used magazines. Despite that fortress of an entrance that had to be opened by skeleton key, we had freedoms here that we didn't have in the US, where Abuelo kept a strict seven o'clock curfew, which didn't really matter much because there was nowhere to go within walking distance. There, we wasted our evenings glued to the television. Back in our homeland, we felt energized by the activity on the plaza, the constant wave of voices. People spilled out of the church and crowded around the women roasting nuts or pumpkin seeds on large metal discs. Musicians competed against the politicians speaking through ear-piercing sound systems. Groups of teenagers teased each other with flirtatious dares, and the younger kids chased stray dogs out to the street. This was familiar territory. What we had given up. Yet we convinced ourselves, perhaps because we could not choose to return, that we were better off in the north, that opportunities awaited us that none of these people swirling about the plaza could even imagine. At one point, as we walked by a young man our age who was setting up his shoe shine kit on the steps of the church courtyard, my brother turned to me and said, "That would've been us if we had stayed."

I was surprised to hear that insight coming from my younger brother. I was even more startled by the fact that I agreed with him, that somehow we had found a silver lining in the loss of our homeland and the loss of our mother. Sacrifice. That was the word Abuela used often. Sacrifice is what it took to achieve a reward. I imagined that's how my family justified our migration north. I imagined that's what Adelina had also been told when she agreed to join us. Any suffering would be worth it in the end.

At night, Alex and I snuggled into our individual beds and watched television programming in Spanish, something we had access to in the US but which we didn't care for. We were too busy assimilating with MTV and thirty-minute sitcoms about silly white people who got a laugh for stubbing a toe. We didn't say much to each other because there was nothing to share. The only time we broached anything close to a serious conversation was when we wondered why Tía Sara lived like a wealthy Mexican with a bountiful kitchen and two servant girls who washed the bedsheets every other day, while we lived in the US as poor people.

"She probably married money," I concluded.

Whatever the reason, the courtyard was filled with wonder—a fig tree that exploded with fruit every morning, a flock of cooing doves that shed downy feathers into the air, and a Doberman pinscher with its tail cut off that answered to the name of Hitler. Tía Sara seemed embarrassed to tell us this, but she had no choice. Calling out its name was the only way to quiet the animal.

"My youngest named him that," she explained. "And the name stuck. It's vulgar I know, but what can we do?"

Hitler was a gentle animal most of the time, but his bark was frightening. And because I reminded him of his young owner (or so my aunt said), it gravitated toward me especially. If I stood or sat down, the dog would press its lean but sturdy body against my legs, threatening to knock me off balance.

A week into our visit, Alex and I had grown accustomed to our newfound perks and privileges, so that it was with great disappointment that we received the news from Abuela that we were headed back to California. "So gather your things," she said. Alex and I stuffed our duffel bags with clothes and the small collection of knickknacks we had accumulated on our daily trips to the plaza. Another two-day journey was upon us.

A few hours later, Abuelo instructed us to hop inside the camper. When I picked up my duffel bag he yelled out, "Leave that there, stupid. We're going to run some errands first."

My heart sank. That nastiness was just a glimpse of the company we were going to keep all the way back home. An hour later, as we pulled into El Pueblito, Abuelo told us to stay put inside the camper. Minutes later the camper door opened and we sat there speechless and confused as a frightened young woman climbed in with us.

"That's Adelina," Abuelo said. "Your cousin. She's going to take care of you." And then the camper door slammed shut.

The whole episode was something out of a kidnapping plot. The visit was no longer than a few minutes and the young woman had climbed on board without even a purse, just the clothes on her back—a pink hand-knitted sweater, a plain blue skirt, and white knee-high socks with holes in them. As Abuelo drove back to Zacapu, the young woman began to hyperventilate. Alex and I simply watched, uncertain about what to do.

"You have a cut there," Alex pointed out to her, finally breaking the awkward silence.

We all looked down at her hand. Her fingernail was bleeding. I knew that kind of damage—evidence of a desperate grip in a hard-fought battle that had just been lost.

That rest of the afternoon was surreal. Abuelo employed a soft, almost tender manner when speaking to Adelina. Unsettling at first, it eventually angered me because I knew this act was short-lived, that by the time we arrived back in California he would resort back to his brutish ways.

We stopped at the mercado, which puzzled me because I didn't think there was any need for grocery shopping, but then we bee-lined it to the back of the building, where the merchants sold cheap clothing. Since Adelina climbed into the truck without a suitcase, this would have to do for the moment. Abuela coaxed her into choosing a blouse, stockings, and underwear, which was stuffed into a cone made from newspaper. Even during this intimate selection she remained stoic, in shock, so I became embarrassed for her at the indignity of having to pick her panty colors in front of all of us.

"Would you like an ice cream?" Abuelo said in his fake gentle voice.

Adelina nodded, a glimmer of excitement on her face, and this is when I realized how young she actually was. She picked a tamarind ice cream bar and devoured it, as if this was the last taste of anything she was going to have of her homeland. I remembered that sense of impending separation when I had to climb on a bus with my family to travel north to the border three years before. I wanted to hold on to something—a final touch, a final taste, a last-chance encounter that I could brand into my brain as the parting gift from my beloved hometown.

As we sat in silence consuming our treats I finally wondered about Adelina, how her name sounded eerily similar to my mother's—Avelina—how her presence here seemed more like a penance than a reward. Had she done something to offend her family who so willingly offered her up for this task of being a nanny to two orphans living in California? Had she been told earlier that week or was she informed just hours ago? The fact that she had been flung into the truck like an exile suggested other dramatic explanations. Had she sinned against her body? Had she sinned against God? She looked so innocent and fragile, I couldn't imagine what her story was, and I had a feeling I would never find out.

When we got back to Tía Sara, who kept shaking her head with disapproval, Adelina withdrew even deeper into herself, lowering her head as if in shame. Tía Sara's two servant girls kept eyeing her from a distance as they moved about doing their chores. And then Adelina's situation worsened when Abuelo sat her down in a chair in the middle of the courtyard and cut off her long hair. I became mortified at that public display of humiliation, at the way Tía Sara kept verbalizing her disbelief in what was happening, and how the two servant girls started to giggle, sticking out their tongues at Adelina who had just aged a few decades after Abuela combed her hair to look exactly like hers—short and with the bangs combed back.

I walked up to Abuela and asked her discreetly, "Why did he cut it off?"

Abuela put her finger to her lips and then pointed with her eyes at a white bucket with Adelina's discarded hair. I bent down to look at it and recognized the infestation of lice. Meanwhile, Adelina simply sat there, expressionless and defeated.

"Why don't you start looking after the boys now," Abuelo told Adelina. She got up from her seat and followed Alex and me to the fig tree at the end of the courtyard. She watched over Alex with disinterest as he climbed up to pick fruit.

Even from a distance I could hear the grown-ups laughing about the whole situation. I felt I needed to counter that laughter with some compassion, so I started to ask questions.

"You like figs?" I said, offering her one that Alex had pelted down from the tree.

She took it in her hand but it was more like an act of obedience.

"Have you ever been to California?" I asked and then realized what a stupid thing that was to say. But I was at a loss. I didn't know how to reach out to her. Adelina was a distant cousin, a member of the cheese-makers from El Pueblito, so what in the world was she doing getting herself involved with this depressing side of the family? That's the question I really wanted to ask.

But once she realized that I had given up trying to engage her, she spoke up on her own.

"My mother's sick," she said softly. I hardly recognized her voice. All this time she had been nodding her head or answering my grandparents in monosyllables.

"My mother died," I said, and for the first time since she was thrown into the truck we made eye contact. Her eyes became watery. I wasn't sure if she was grieving for herself or for me, or for both of us, but I was strangely comforted by the fact that I had someone near me who knew about such pain. My younger brother Alex had been refusing to talk about our mother's death. Whenever I brought it up he would stiffen and say, "Can we change the conversation?" or "I don't want to talk about that." So even though we had suffered the same loss I felt alone all this time. Suddenly, I began to imagine that it wouldn't be so bad to have Adelina among us. Her role was to be our nanny, but there would be a special connection between us, as if she had come into my life to be the older sibling I desperately needed—someone to protect *me* for a change from the awful things of this world, like death, like school bullies, like Abuelo.

"Why don't we go to the plaza together one last time?" Alex called out from the fig tree. And I thought what a great idea it would be to say goodbye to Zacapu together, just the three of us. But when I asked Abuelo for permission, he shot it down.

"She can't leave the house," he said. "If you want to go, you go alone, but don't stay out too late. We leave at the crack of dawn."

I wanted to stay behind to keep Adelina company, but my brother wasn't having it and pleaded with me to come along; otherwise he would not be allowed to venture out by himself. And in truth, I wanted to go out as well. So we left Adelina perched on the stone border around the fig tree and I promised myself that I would bring her something back. When we got to the front door, Tía Sara came over with her skeleton key and unlocked it, as usual. That's when I realized that Adelina was a prisoner. That she was not allowed to come with us because my grandparents were afraid she would escape.

"I don't understand," I said to Alex. "Are we forcing her to go with us?"

"I think so," Alex said.

My goodbye stroll along the plaza was sullied by the thought of Adelina getting smaller and smaller as the hour of our departure neared. And suddenly I began to question whether I really wanted to return. What if I fled that very moment and hid away with my mother's relatives? They were church people, kind of boring and not very expressive, but they weren't mean or abusive like Abuelo. I thought about proposing the idea to Alex but I didn't dare. Even then I knew what a stupid risk it was, and what dire consequences awaited us after Abuelo claimed us back.

Before returning to Tía Sara's I bought Adelina a set of barrettes. It seemed like an insensitive gift but Abuela had pinned Adelina's hair back with those old-lady bobby pins that had aged her. We knocked on Tía Sara's door and we heard her unlocking like a warden.

"Did you have a nice time?" she asked, and I wanted to spit on her. Surely she could see what a cruel thing was taking place right in her own house, and though she kept muttering her disapproval, she was going to do nothing to stop her stubborn older brother.

As the grown-ups prepared the final meal in the kitchen their mood was celebratory. Laughter and music lit up the small room while just a few feet away Adelina sulked in a chair. I walked up to her with my gift.

"I brought you these," I said, holding up the barrettes. But instead of taking them, she took hold of my wrist.

"You have to help me," she said. Her eyes were burning with anxiety.

"Help you how?" I said. Though I knew exactly what she was asking.

Adelina pulled me so close to her that for a moment I thought she was going to kiss me, but I didn't resist. And just as I was about to anticipate our faces coming together she froze, her eyes locked directly with mine.

A flash of recognition passed between us, and in that instant I began to suspect why she had been cast out of her family, her village, why she was being punished like this. There it was, that thing inside of me that made me different, an aberration in the eyes of family and an insult to God. Or maybe that was wishful thinking, me projecting my own fears upon this young woman who was opening her soul to me, trusting me while she was at her most vulnerable. In any case, I responded in kind, revealing my true self, letting her in on this secret that I wanted someone else to recognize without ridicule or disgust.

Suddenly, I became even more frightened. What if I denied her? Would she betray me? Would she confirm for Abuelo what he was probably suspecting all along and would he then cast me out of this family as well, maybe drop me off in El Pueblito on our way out because that would be an apt punishment for me—a life of labor in a rural village that would butch me up, me this sissy of a boy who was all sentimentality and sensitivity, not much of a man-to-be at all.

"Will you help me?" This time she appealed to me with a kindness in her voice that convinced me she was intending no malice. So I resolved to help her.

I'd be lying if I didn't admit that I was experiencing a thrill plotting Adelina's flight. But it was a relatively easy plan to come up with and execute. I wandered into the kitchen the way young people sometimes do, curious about the goings-on with the grown-ups until one of them shooed the underaged visitor away from the off-color jokes and big-people talk. I was able to sneak in and out without notice, pinching Tía Sara's skeleton key, which she kept in plain sight and which remained forgotten until it was needed.

Adelina was already waiting in the shadows. The music was playing loud enough that it would drown out the creaking of the door opening. But just as we started to fiddle with the lock in the dark, Hitler came barking. Adelina cowered in the corner and whimpered in fear.

"It's okay, it's okay," I said.

I called the dog over. It recognized me and started to press against my legs to show its affection. This time I didn't push it away. This time I needed to keep the animal tame. I continued to jiggle the key in the lock until it finally clicked open. A puff of fresh air blew in from the street. I looked at Adelina who looked incredulous that we had gone this far. She hesitated.

"What's the matter?" I said. Suddenly I worried that this pause in the plan was going to cost us. I felt the heat of Abuelo's belt across my ass.

Even in the shadow I saw the glossy glare of Adelina's eyes. She had been moved by my actions. And just as easily my own eyes began to water. The moment seemed inappropriately melodramatic, maybe even unconvincing because we had just met a few hours ago and here we were weeping at our parting. But we were both in states of distress—I had lost my loved one and she had been rejected by hers. We were both abandoned and alone, and possibly, just maybe, or so I wanted to believe, we were both struggling with our sexual identities. She was my sister in that moment and I was her brother, and we had just found each other but now we were saying goodbye. And for a moment I thought about going with her, about escaping into the night in order to live my own life, not the one that was being dictated by family. I pictured taking her hand and stepping through the threshold right after her, shutting the door behind us and disappearing into who knows what wondrous freedoms. But before I had a chance to take this moment of fantasy any further, Adelina flew out like the caged dove that she was, her pink sweater suddenly bright and magical. I watched her turn the corner and I imagined her slipping into a whole new dimension where she would remain safe—untouched and unharmed—for the rest of her days.

Solemnly, I closed the door to Adelina's courageous world and shut myself inside my own. I couldn't walk out, not just yet, not with my little brother Alex to look after. I turned the lock and stepped back inside my family's suffocating reverie.

Achy Obejas

The Maldives

As soon as I was diagnosed with a brain tumor, I knew I wanted to be here, in the Maldives. My tumor is benign, at least technically, just a little drop of fat, not cancerous. It's growing about one centimeter a year, which is about the same as the rising sea level in the Maldives. But this coincidence isn't what drew me to these islands.

For me, everything started just before I left Cuba. I'd just scored an American visa because my father, who'd escaped years before on a raft, had filed for me under a family reunification provision of US asylum laws. Not that my father had much interest in being reunited with me: When he lived in Cuba, he never hesitated to tell me I was a punishment from God.

I'd ask him, For what? What did you do to deserve me? It must have been pretty bad.

But he'd just shake his head and walk away. I'm not going to confess to you, he'd spit over his shoulder.

Years later, all settled in San Francisco with a new Mexican wife and a revved-up religious calling that involved marching up and down Market Street passing out pamphlets urging homosexuals to repent, he decided maybe God would be more convinced of his commitment and sacrifice if he saved his own daughter first.

And I was ready to be saved. Not from homosexuality but from the boredom of Havana. Oh, I know, most Americans hear Havana and think Tropicana and classic cars, parties and salsa, even though salsa is Puerto Rican. But for a Cuban like me, Havana means living with several generations in a crowded three-room apartment (in my case, my mother, her boyfriend, my grandmother and her boyfriend, my sister and her boyfriend, my nineteen-year-old nephew and his boyfriend, and his boyfriend's two-year-old son), a job during the day earning worthless pesos (I was a security guard at the Museum of Fine Arts), and a job at night earning hard currency (I washed dishes at a fancy family-run restaurant, a position I got by marrying—that's right, marrying—the owner because Cuban law demands that family businesses only hire family). My Havana was dirty and teeming, and so loud it sometimes felt like a piercing in my ears. I honestly could not remember the last time I'd been alone for more than it takes to relieve myself, and even then I wasn't immune to the soundtrack of screaming and clattering.

Given my age—thirty-four—and my situation, I'd already been with pretty much everybody I was going to be with in Havana. And given how overcrowded we were at home (I slept in the same sweat-drenched bed with my nephew, his boyfriend, and their two-year-old, or, weather permitting, on a hammock I'd strung up that ran parallel with the clothesline on the tenement's back patio), I knew nobody was going to move in with me, even if she loved me, and I wasn't sure I brought enough to the table, in spite of my dollar-earning dishwashing job, to be wanted enough to take home. In the few instances when the possibility arose, it was only because the other girl's overcrowded home mirrored mine, but with an additional half dozen cousins from the provinces. That only left tourists as romantic possibilities and, though my English is fine, nothing calmed my ardor quicker than some American telling me all about the wonders of the revolution as she paid my way into a dollars-only club I would otherwise not be able to afford.

In fact, I was celebrating the visa my father had gotten me at precisely one of those clubs, listening to a pretty terrible reggaeton band whose terribleness was underscored by a terrible sound system, when I experienced the tumor's first overt symptom. In an instant, the bass just dropped out of the music. It became tinny and thin. Because the sound quality at all Havana venues—even the very best ones—is unpredictable, I was sure it had nothing to do with me. I was with a bunch of friends, typical Cubans, and a Canadian who was being hustled by one of those friends and had paid for all of us. I shrugged an apology her way and she smiled uncertainly in my direction.

When we left a few hours later, my left ear felt plugged. A loud argument was taking place as we passed a cafe, and a drunk blared a trumpet at the corner, but they sounded gauzy and far away.

Oh, I know that feeling: my ears got waterlogged when I went diving in the Maldives, the Canadian said.

Everybody nodded as if they knew the exact coordinates of the Maldives, afraid to seem ignorant in front of the Canadian, but I wondered if it wasn't one of those countries where Cuba had sent medical brigades. I was pretty sure I'd seen something in a documentary; Cuban TV is one long parade of documentaries. In any case, I hadn't been diving, ever, in my whole life, but I did wonder, immediately, if going deep underwater meant peace and solitude or if all those schools of fish and shivers of sharks made you feel just as crowded as the city and maybe even a little paranoid.

Do you have hydrogen peroxide at home? the Canadian asked. Pour some in your ear—it'll sound like fireworks—and then lay on your side and it'll clear up.

But it didn't, and I suspect it wouldn't have even if we'd had hydrogen peroxide. In fact, during the next few days my hearing seemed to fluctuate wildly. Most of the time, it felt as if everything was at a great distance, as if everyone was talking to me from the bottom of the sea. My mother told me she thought it was stress, and that seemed a reasonable explanation. After all, I was leaving soon, headed to the great unknown of the United States, and though I wasn't planning on living with my father, technically I did have to stay with him for a year and a day because he was sponsoring me. I hadn't seen him in more than a decade; I hadn't heard his voice in almost that long, when he'd called out of the blue to say he wanted to save me. My mother said it must all be happening for a reason.

My hearing got no better as I prepped for my trip, but by the time I was ready to go, I must have gotten used to it because I wasn't paying attention to it anymore. Then, as I was getting on the plane, waving at my family waving at me from the tarmac—my grandmother's boyfriend has a relative who's a high-ranking airport official so they all got to personally escort me to the plane—I felt a twitching in my left eye. I'd been very sad, especially as I waved at my grandmother wondering if I'd ever see her again, but I hadn't been able to cry, or, more precisely, to cry in any kind of recognizable fashion. My right eye teared but my left remained stoic. And now this: little electrical flashes flaring across my eyeball. Because, you see, it was in my eyeball—not on my eyelid, not on my brow—but right there, in my eye, as if my retina had developed a tick. For a few minutes, I saw double and I had difficulty climbing the airstairs and finding my seat. Everyone assumed I was just too emotional to make sense of boarding.

But the twitching didn't go away. At customs in Miami, it got so bad I was actually asked by an agent if I needed medical attention. I said I didn't, that I was just nervous about my new life, which my trembling hands seemed to authenticate. What had me genuinely concerned was that my left eye now felt as if someone was constantly opening and shutting a set of blinds. I was supposed to have two hours of rest before I caught my next flight to San Francisco but, assuming it was the prospect of seeing my father that had triggered my state, I quickly pulled out my contact list—the list every Cuban has of who they'll call if they ever get off the island—and asked a passenger from my flight if I could borrow her cell phone. I tried to calm down enough to dial.

One of the advantages of my worthless museum security guard job was that I got to meet a lot of foreigners, especially artists. They were usually busy proving their proletariat bona fides to the other Cubans—who never talked to us—by making nice with guards and janitors and such. That's how I'd gotten to know a video artist named Laura Vaas when she had a one-woman show at the museum. During her installation, it'd frequently been just her and me through many an afternoon, and I'd proven a good helper and sounding board. Before she left Cuba, she'd given me her number and said to call her if I ever found myself in Miami.

"This is who again?" Laura asked after I'd identified myself. The volume was up high enough that the phone's owner heard her and looked at me with concern.

I told her my name again. "From the museum in Havana."

To my surprise, Laura didn't hesitate once I explained about my father the avenging Christian and the way my body had gone into revolt at the thought of seeing him. In about an hour she was exactly where she said she'd be, at the Starbucks in Terminal D East just outside the security check. I've never been so relieved in my life; I honestly don't know what I would have done if she hadn't shown up. The flicker in my eye had sped up to about a mile a minute while I waited.

Laura greeted me with a familiar hug that far exceeded our island acquaintance, took my single suitcase, and drove me to her home, which turned out to be not a palace on the beach but a small wooden house in Kendall with a garage that served as her studio. I almost asked her what had happened, that I thought she was a successful artist, but I caught myself: She was driving a 2002 Ford Focus station wagon. By Cuban standards, that's practically a luxury car but I knew, even in the airport parking lot where it was surrounded by scores of newer, shinier cars I could only rightfully picture through my one good eye, that I'd probably misjudged her situation.

That very night, after settling me into her guest bedroom, Laura gave me a spare laptop—a spare laptop!—and set up an account for me on Facebook. She suggested I try to find people I knew in the States. I told her about my contact list but she said on Facebook all you needed was somebody's name, that I didn't need their phone number or address. I sat at the kitchen table long after she went to bed, one hand covering my jittery eye, and the other typing in name after name of people I knew from Cuba who'd been long gone.

I was on an old friend's page when I saw some pictures of myself from the very night my ear had started giving me trouble. There I was dancing, though you could see from my expression something was wrong. Then I noticed the Canadian was also in the frame. My friend had tagged her and I followed the link to her page where I discovered there was a whole album—132 total pictures—of her trip to Cuba, including many of places I'd never even heard of, like a beach called Maria La Gorda that had been declared a World Biosphere Reserve by UNESCO. This was a Cuba unknown to me: all parrotfish and blurry hummingbirds, with only the occasional brown arm helping the Canadian onto a boat or serving her and her friends a bountiful meal.

I scanned her other albums and saw she was quite the world traveler: swimming with green sea turtles in the Philippines and with moray eels in the Solomon Islands, and walking along what appeared to be a beach at night with blue-white stars scattered in the sand, as if the sky had emptied a constellation on the shore. I wondered if my eye was playing tricks on me. The caption read: Ostracod crustaceans, kind of like bioluminescent phytoplankton, lighting up the shore on Mudhdhoo Island in the Maldives. I thought: Wow.

I stayed up close to dawn searching for more photos of this strange phenomenon but mostly finding image after image of beaches and beach towns in the Maldives: little storybook villages with an infinite span of blue-green water surrounding them, the sky an endless and tender light. Nothing looked crowded in the Maldives, and even in the capital city of Malé, houses were wreathed by gardens of blue and orange flowers, hammocks everywhere. Best of all, of the approximately twelve hundred islands that make up the country—and I say approximately because the number of islands depends on the season—only about two hundred are inhabited, and only half of those have tourist resorts. Honestly, I couldn't figure out why UNESCO hadn't declared all the Maldives a World Biosphere Reserve.

The next day, I opened my eyes and everything was in perfect focus: The ceiling fan above Laura's guest bed, the floral print on the duvet, the giant black screen on the wall with its blinking red light. It took me a second to remember where I was—the United States, Miami, the home of someone I barely knew—and then I heard a low bass throbbing through the wall and the sharp knock of Laura's knuckles on the bedroom door.

Adelante, I said, and in she came with a tray holding a glass of orange juice, a banana, a stack of pancakes and a small cup of black coffee with a full head of foam.

You won't get service like this every day, she said, but today being your first day in America . . .

I almost said something about America being the entirety of the western hemisphere but gratitude shut me up. Instead I asked her how to make the picture of the glow-in-the-dark beach in the Maldives the wallpaper on my new laptop.

In truth, Laura Vaas turned out to be an exceptional friend. When I further explained my situation—including that I wouldn't have a green card or a work permit for a year and a day—she got on the phone and found me a job washing dishes at a restaurant owned by some friends of hers who paid me in cash. She also got me odd jobs with other artists packing work for shipping. I wasn't making a ton of money but enough to buy a bus pass, go to a movie now and again, and buy groceries and creams for my chapped hands. Then Laura said she was going on a fellowship to London for part of the year and would have had to pay someone to housesit if I hadn't shown up. My free housing would continue, so even though I was sending money to my family every month, I was even able to start saving.

I did get a cell phone pretty quickly, and I did eventually call my father and thank him for getting me out of Cuba. He was furious with me, accused me of using him just to come over, but I made no effort to explain how I'd gotten sick just thinking about living with him. Part of it was that, as time had passed and my vision and hearing returned to normal, it was hard to believe my symptoms hadn't been psychosomatic, and I just didn't want to give him that kind of power.

In spite of having my new cell, I didn't make other calls. I knew people in Miami and Key West and Tampa, but I actually didn't want to see anyone. I folded up my contact list and put it away. Laura's house was blissfully quiet—all I ever heard were little warblers up in the palm trees and the mailman lifting the letter slot in the afternoon. My bed, which Laura constantly apologized for because it was only a single, felt as long and wide as a luxury liner to me.

Initially, I had tried to pay Laura back for her kindness by cooking and cleaning but she got upset, said she was gaining weight, and that she liked to take care of her stuff herself. I was terrified I'd offended her so I just tried to stay out of her way and holed up in the guest room. I watched a lot of TV on the big screen in my room, especially documentaries, including

The Island President, about how the Maldives are disappearing due to rising sea levels caused by climate change. The Maldivian president wants the world to learn a lesson from his country's predicament. He wants the world to take responsibility. The situation is so bad they've even got a sovereign land fund to buy new territory and move once their country's submerged, like Alexandria and the pyramids of Yonaguni in Japan. Or like Guanahacabibes, an underwater city off Cuba's western shore, except no one who isn't Cuban actually thinks it's a city, just a bunch of geological anomalies.

As soon as Laura left for London, I ended my self-imposed exile in the guest room. I opened every door in the house and danced from room to room. What splendor to open my arms wide and just feel cool satiny air conditioning on my skin. What extravagance to take a hot forty minute shower in the morning and a cool hour long bath at night. I walked around naked and whistled and even did cartwheels in the living room.

I thought for sure I'd grow lonesome at some point but I didn't. I got plenty of human interaction at the restaurant and on the bus. Every now and again I'd run into someone I knew and when I evaded their questions they assumed I was either having a mysterious affair with a rich American or spying for Cuba. They'd write my mother and then she'd write me and I know we both laughed about it.

One night at the restaurant, I was loading the dishwasher and singing along to a new song by Calle 13 when suddenly somebody turned off the radio. Hey, I said, c'mon, as I reached for a pair of latex gloves to tackle the pots. But the music didn't come back on. I walked over to the radio and turned up the dial and almost immediately one of the owners swatted my hand away. He was saying something—his mouth was moving and his face showed irritation—but I couldn't hear a thing. I shook my head but the bubble tightened: Suddenly I could only see him through what appeared to be a fish-eye lens. He grabbed me by the shoulders and brought his face close to mine but I couldn't understand him.

Before I knew it, the other owner, a Panamanian guy who had been trying to set me up with his fifty-two-year-old sister since I'd arrived, threw me in his Jeep and drove me to the emergency room at Jackson Memorial Hospital. We were there until dawn and he stayed with me the whole time, occasionally squeezing my hand and bringing me something to eat and drink. The ER wasn't much different than Ciro Garcia in Havana, except that the electricity didn't go out the whole time we were there. Otherwise, it was the same defeated faces, the same resignation to whatever fate had just been ordained by a fall or accident or, in my case, a sudden short circuit.

They found the tumor when they did an MRI of my brain. It sat dead center in my skull, shaped like a two-inch comma leaning heavily to the left. It had wrapped itself around my auditory nerve so as to practically strangle it. It was also big enough to damage both cranial nerves four and five, which explained why I'd had double vision and couldn't tear up. What they couldn't tell me was why I had hearing loss in both ears. They needed to run more tests. Unless I did something, they said via notes the Panamanian wrote out in his boxy script, both my hearing and vision would slowly deteriorate. They talked about surgery and radiation, experimental medicines and treatments like the cyber knife and auditory brain implants, all of which I could never afford. The restaurant didn't offer health insurance and I would have been ineligible anyway, waiting for the year and a day when I would have my US residence and my work permit. I wasn't dying, and I wouldn't die from this tumor, they told me, but left alone it would eventually leave me trapped in my own body.

After the Panamanian took me home, I sat in Laura's expansive living room and thought about my predicament. My father would tell me this was a punishment from God for all my sins, for all the women I'd briefly loved. My mother would tell me it was destiny, that there are forces in the universe greater than us that we simply must obey. Was there anything to learn, for anyone, from my situation? Who would take responsibility for me?

I got myself a beer from Laura's fridge and counted my money. I had saved about eight thousand dollars. I was considering buying a ticket back to Havana, knowing with that money my family could probably take care of me for a very long time. I had no illusions about my condition being relieved in Havana. Certainly, I would get medical attention, I would be visited by doctors. But I knew Cuba simply didn't have the equipment or expertise to help me. And I didn't want to have brain surgery at a hospital where the power went off and on without regard to what was happening on the operating table.

I opened my laptop to send an email to an acquaintance from the museum who had agreed to relay messages to my mother in case of emergency. When I saw my wallpaper, that blue-white constellation across the coastline in the Maldives, I knew time was of the essence. I might not ever hear the waves lapping the shore but my vision, at least at that moment, was again as good as a high-powered Leica lens. When I searched for one-way tickets to Malé, I found they were within my reach. In the weeks following my arrival, I found a job washing dishes. I figure I can do that, or maybe gardening, until my eyes fail. Then I will sail to one of those islands where no one goes and lay myself down in all that phosphorescence. I will sink into the firmament of the Maldives one centimeter at a time and let the waters rise, lifting me, guiding me through the silent dark to my own Atlantis.

Annie Finch

Letter to Shahid Ali, in a Warm September

For Agha Shahid Ali, 1949-2001

Sometimes it seems I'll never get back to sleeping like that again—like the simple way that my mother
led me to sleep as a child, with a Scottish sleep
song about sheepfolds to quiet my bones. That's the sleep
I hope you struck off for on your last journey, Shahid.
You were younger than my age now. Why shouldn't your sleep
be sweet, like your waking was—a wide, strong child's sleep?
Isn't it true that any poet who could write a canzone
as veiled and loving, as thick and crying, a canzone
as clear and dying as yours are, deserves to sleep?
To repeat (we know) takes, and gives, innocence—so kiss
me goodnight again, dear duende Shahid. Let the bursting kiss

of your words buoy up my own; leave me a kiss
of my own, to own my words. Then, at last, I'll sleep.
Because what are poet's voices, after all, but kisses alert and awake in the mouth, heartbeats's soul-kiss-
es glistening as far past touch as the memory a mother
trails like mica in the rock-making dust of our loneliest kiss?
Though you taught me something, once, about how rhymed words kiss
(the gift you said that Merrill had given to you once, Shahid),
no rhymes need weight this floating gift you left me, Agha Shahid
Ali—this vessel your poems still weave—this boat that will kiss
the sky till it rains—this excrescent, exuberant canzone—
this life raft for poets on watery journeys. Ah, canzone,

you squeeze like a jellyfish, you weep like a pine tree, you, canzone,
lick me long as the endless tongue of a dangerous kiss.
Shahid, how could you have kissed us with anything but a canzone
(no, three! And it seems that the tracks of a canzone
are fertile, like the tracks of a night with little sleep . . .)
Ah, Shahid, would you have left us anything but a canzone?
It trailed after you from your deathbed, your last canzone,
the mysterious one. Then there was the great one about your mother,
which you wrote while she was dying. And now my mother
may soon be dying, and finally I float this canzone
out on the waves that you make rock for me, Shahid,
veiling the air with such moving water, Shahid,

canzone, canzone, Shahid, face, Shahid, voice, memory, the Shahid
we poets repeat now, insistent as a canzone:
"Shahid was so witty. Oh, how I miss Shahid. Ah, Shahid . . ."
"No one cooked (entertained, laughed, spoke) like him . . ." Ah, Shahid,
you "the beloved" ("the witness" in Arabic) whose name-kiss
winks out from so many ghazals that the name "Shahid"
becomes its admirers, you're a rare poet still, still-rocking Shahid.
It's a sweet veil (you know it) that reaches out from such hard-rocking sleep,
trailing us in, in to the births that will trail neither sleep
nor forgetting, but trail births again. A poet as full as you, Shahid,
comes into a life like a witness. When I saw the words "Agha Shahid
Ali Reading, February 26" on the email, I was the raw mother
of a two-month-old, influenced mainly by my mother—

a poet whose voice felt alone. How could I have known, Shahid,
that you'd be with me even now still, standing near my grandmother
where she's been smiling for decades out of the gathering of souls? Oh Mother
Goddess! What a gift, your poet's dear voice, dear poet! Each canzone,
smile, ghazal, joke, protest, villanelle. The thick pollen of the Mother
of Muses sifted on you so deeply (she's memory, memory, mother
also of madness, and grieving, and joy, remember?) She had scattered her kiss
over us, eight years before, with our friendship's first kiss,
2 a.m. at the poetry conference when you named me (a first-time new mother,

first time away from my baby, not eager to sleep),
then baptized my name with your voice, as welcome as sleep,

and mocked how Americans pronounce it. And then, I could sleep,
since you spoke it as no one had done all my life but my mother,
linking us forever that night. Teacher. Mother. Oh Shahid.
Name giver. Rhyme keeper. Ghazal shaper. Bearer of the canzone,
I touch you to life with a poem now, one more—late, like a kiss.

Wendy Barker

Surgery, A Little History

Stunned by the god's "feathered glory," Yeats
    said of Leda. How many painters have rendered this
        image, of a woman swooning with a swan. The trickery,
the deceit of Zeus, disguising himself. And these
    doctors, their downy reassurance. Robotic surgery,
        they coo, easy as slipping into and out of a pond. Not
gods, but white-coated, so feathery-voiced
    I believe them, sign the forms. Their sleek offices,
        paintings of lakes, of cool streams on their walls. Such
calming waters I lie back, feet propped in the metal
    stirrups, till the speculum is pressed inside, probing
        for what lies underneath: stems of water lilies, small
fish. Scraping the silt. No "sudden blow,"
    the surgeons promise, "minimally invasive, laparoscopic,
        tiny incisions, needle-thin instruments. Nothing to fear,"
they stress. But photos I've now seen online
    show massive silvery cones, spiked bills that angle
        like spears toward the bull's-eye of a belly. "Indifferent"
beaks that peck around inside, pulling sagging
    organs upright, shoving them into new places,
        wrapping them in mesh like the webs between toes
of swans. "A month," they said. But it's more
    like ten before my body's mine again, works again,
        though I'm told I'm a lucky one, patients half my age
may need a catheter for a year, even
    two, "post-op," and often, they add, women will
        need the surgery redone. We say we're "put under" an

anesthetic. And how I've gone under, sunk
　　　down into the murk to remember the time during
　　　　　　eighth grade when my mother picked me up, surprising
me after school, my gray Samsonite packed in
　　　the Ford's back seat: "We're going to the hospital,
　　　　　　honey, just a little operation, so you won't have those
awful cramps anymore." After the nurse stripped me
　　　and tied me into a blue robe that left my bottom bare,
　　　　　　she told my mother to leave. They swooped in then,
medical students, checking for cancer,
　　　they said, and pulled aside the gown, fingered
　　　　　　my breasts. In the morning, the nurse wheeled me
down the hall for the little operation. The doctor
　　　and his white-jacketed flock were waiting, thought
　　　　　　the anesthetic had kicked in. I was awake all during
their hooting, their laughing. Spread-eagled in
　　　the stirrups, the clamp inside, the scraping. No
　　　　　　Yeatsian "white rush." The blood that followed. My
mother never knew. Shortly before she
　　　died, she told me how, the first year she was
　　　　　　married, her doctor insisted she come to the office
Saturday morning. Got her on her back, fiddled
　　　with her clitoris, diddled her, his fingers pulsing
　　　　　　inside her, experimenting, to make her come. The same
ob/gyn who delivered me, who believed
　　　women should suffer in childbirth, no need
　　　　　　for an anesthetic while he rammed those forceps deep
inside to haul me out. The body holds these
　　　incisions. For years. And genetic memory
　　　　　　exists: we carry molecular scars. No eggs from such
visitations. Only hard-boiled knowledge
　　　that you won't get the truth from these
　　　　　　hook-scissored beaks when what they do is tear, rip
into you, and maybe, maybe, you'll recover, put on
　　　new knowledge with your own power. Flap back at
　　　　　　them, beat your own wings against them. And snap.

Margaret Randall

When Justice Felt at Home

Something has changed.
Only old friends,
those who shared split peas
and white rice
on sweltering Havana nights
still call me *compañera*:
sweet designation
meaning comrade or friend
lover or familiar
in those luminous days
when justice felt at home
in our desire.

Now, more often than not,
it's *señora*:
regression to a prehistory
when married or single
young or old
mattered most.

Still, *compañera* and *compañero*
are indelibly embossed
on the swaying trunks of Royal Palms,
in Sierra Maestra granite
and along the dissembling coastline
of an Island that still shouts freedom
into gale-force winds.

Ron Paul Salutsky

Elegy with a Heart-Shaped Box

I wish I'd realized then
everything before us

would soon be an after,
that day in middle May,

the week's work finished
for a minute, we rode the bike

first to Wakulla Springs
then to Whataburger,

took the choice table
by the window looking under

the giant live oak on the square,
so old it must've been shade

for freed slaves at one time,
then the two kids, maybe an older

and younger brother, sat down behind me,
talking loud about a video game

or snot or boobies, kicking the bench
I sat on, my dirty look

first at you and then at them, thinking
we must move, or tell them

the waitress sprayed poison
cleaning chemicals on that table

and if they didn't want their arms
to rot off, they'd be wise to find

a different table, during the few seconds
the sun-deepened freckles on your cheeks

struck me in a slant of light,

their number was called,
and the taller got up, walked over

to the counter where the lady
in the orange jumpsuit and apron

handed him a medium-looking box
of fries, and he walked to the door,

saying nothing, cupping the box

just in front of his heart
as if it held an injured wren

the two of them had managed to corral,
and the smaller boy, saying nothing, too,

himself injured and limping a little,

reached across his and his brother's body
for the box, not so much from hunger

as from desire always to have those same things
his bigger brother possesses, and someday,

when one succumbs
to an impossibly early heart attack

or gets t-boned by a college girl
texting her way into a red-light

intersection, the other will struggle
to remember that Saturday,

long before his brother moved away

to work on an oil rig
off the coast of somewhere

they'd just as soon throw you overboard
as pay you,

when they walked all the way
to Midtown from Voncile Street,

the whole way writing stories
in the air,

with two quarters, eight dimes,
and four pennies

in a pocket to buy a heart-shaped box
of fries they'd finish

before they were even a fourth of the way
back home,

and there would be no marker

for this, maybe no recollection at all,
only the quick swoop then hop

of a crow snatching the burnt end
of a fry dropped on the sidewalk,

and left only with this small act
of living, the one brother

he must be starving now
and either this death or this living on

has made him incomplete forever.

David Crouse

I'm Here

The horse's eyes roll deep and black in pained reverie. That's where Edison's attention falls as he suffers the cold to show the animal a small kindness: on the eyes, or rather, the single right eye, which is not like water and not glass and definitely not ice or any of that pretty stuff but simply itself, a flat flickering thing turned inward to a hidden place where Edison is denied access.

As he strokes the flank the fettled skull pushes forward, ears lowered, searching the air for his touch. But his hand is right there, at its side, and the lurching head motion reminds him of a drunk moving back and forth on his heels, but the movement's also more mechanical than that, a heavy shovel edging forward and back. He knows from experience that placing his hand there will stop it but only for a moment before it starts up again, still searching for the touch that's already present. So he strokes the flank and tells the horse sweet words and when those run out, curse words spoken sweetly, because his fingers are getting cold and he wants to be inside in the heat, staring at his computer, just like all those people in the lower forty-eight.

But kindness is a comfort to the one who gives it and work builds character. He needs to tell himself this, he decides, because there is so much of it: two cords of wood to split and stack, a roof that needs shoveling, water to be hauled. The shed would need mending too. The horse's sleek weight had cracked the two-by-fours that first day when he brought it inside, pinched the wall outward, and then the snow had come harder. Each day he stares the task down from a distance, like a sailor falling in love with the sea. He's not ready to throw himself into the midst of it, but he can't pull away.

So he concedes this: first the petting and then the tugging of the wire brush down the horse's neck to its finely muscled shoulder. It's not dying, of course, but it's in a world of hurt. Its hooves have softened and crumbled, first in a simple, almost graceful cleave, and then into a tree of puzzle shapes, spongy to the touch. When he tried touching one in October, when he first noticed, it splashed hot breath in his face, and by mid-November it wouldn't let him touch them at all. Suffering has made the world the animal's enemy. His truck engine makes it start with alarm. The goats come close to the shed and it warns them off with a low, bullish grunt.

Edison isn't sorry though. Buying the horse had not even seemed like a choice so much as an instinct, some nerve twitch that had a flavor of self-preservation to it, like the probing motion of the horse's skull. He would not have been able to live with himself otherwise. The musher, she had stroked its muzzle and said she was going to buy it for dog food, and it took Edison a moment to realize she wasn't joking. The next thing he knew he was doing the math in his head, adding up the money in his savings account, his checking account, in the cigar box on the top shelf in the pantry. The musher begged off, told him if he wanted it that way then fine, she wasn't going to stand in the way of love at first sight. "But that horse isn't worth anything living," she said, as it took the apple core from her open palm.

"You sure you want to do this?" the owner asked him. They had worked together on the roads in Sitka more than a decade before and still maintained a lazy kind of acquaintanceship. Edison had come there to buy some railroad ties—that was all—and maybe have a cup of strong coffee while they talked about the weather, and then there he was, saying sure, of course, as he shook the man's hand. The musher was still there, watching, her flat red face unreadable. Did she think he was a fool? The horse's owner knew Edison's story, or at least the bare bones of it, but that didn't stop him from gripping his hand hard and smiling. "She's good company," he said. "You'll see."

Early December now and he climbs into the loft, attention split between the small window and his computer screen, blanket draped around his shoulders. The window frames the slanted birch trees in the gulley, the haze of stars, and the ice crystals webbed at the corners of the triple pane. The computer screen displays the usual messages from men in the lower forty-eight—in other countries too—describing their bodies, asking him how old he is and where he lives. Alaska, he says, and they ask the standard questions. Isn't it cold there? Lonely there? He tells them the stories they want to hear and soon he *becomes* that person, the person they want him to be, and forgets about the broken shed, the broken hooves.

So many people in the world just want some kind of human connection. They want blowjobs and anal and much more, particular and peculiar things they can describe in minute detail, clinical as surgeons. The red messages blink across the screen, each one demanding his attention. *You must feel like an outsider there*, one of them types, the one who wants to duct tape him from head to toe. *I picture you in Hawaii. I can't picture you there in all that snow. It's like imagining you on the surface of the moon.*

I like it here, he types back, single fingered because his other hand is in his pants.

The man says he just can't picture it. He keeps using the word *picture*, and that's how Edison imagines himself, as a photograph, but not a photograph of himself. He's a snapshot of someone else, one of the pictures he has saved on his hard drive, each figure smiling and young and confident, and when he tells the man to open his mind he feels genuinely offended. After all, Alaska isn't just burly men with beards. But the man is right. Edison *does* feel like an outsider here, because of the color of his skin, or because of the way winter corkscrews itself down into his mind. It's a feeling he's grown to enjoy in an odd way, a kind of raw nakedness. Of course, the girl in each photograph is white. They're always white, and always blonde, and he shares them and says, *My nose looks too big in this one.*

The man almost always says, *You're beautiful.*

The men are all white too, or at least that's how he imagines them, with button-down shirts and receding hairlines and a Coke always on the table. They introduce themselves and then the violent language spills onto his screen, sometimes mixed with sentiment. How quickly they say *I love you* after they've beaten and humiliated him. He's not sure where the fun is in all of this, yet it *is* fun, amazingly so, and when he's finished he goes outside and pees in the snow. But tonight the man doesn't say that he's beautiful. The man, whose screen name is simply *Shyboy*, says, *I've been to Fairbanks. I was in the military there for three years.*

Very cool, Edison says. The blonde girl says it too. She is his puppet, but she's also simply *him*, that part of himself he never named until the Internet made its way to outside the city limits last year and the little dish went up on the side of his place. How did he spend his days before this? When he types the words they come from the deepest, most sincere part of himself. All of them are lies, of course.

Shyboy's history cascades from his fingers. He plays jazz trumpet, was in the Air Force band for years. Lives in Arkansas now. Married twice and has a kid whom he loves deeply. Doesn't get to see him as much as he wants. He's into rape fantasies, forced tattoos, gagging an intelligent young girl with a bright red ball. His boy comes and visits him every other weekend and they always watch a movie together while eating pizza. What to do with all of this? *I have a tattoo*, Edison writes back. *It's on my ankle*.

The outside thermometer stops at twenty-five below.

The horse is in trouble, but it's nothing life threatening, so he turns the key in the ignition for the first time all week and prepares for his trip to town. He lets the engine idle as he picks up summer's trash: a broken plastic chair, stacks of beer bottles, stray wood scraps. It all goes into the truck bed, and soon he's hurling the stuff, throwing it high and letting it fall. The bottles break and the chair clatters. He makes a reckless game of it.

The ice fog begins at Chena Hot Springs Road and he cuts his speed in half, then half again, as he slides down the long hill into the thick of it. He can see the blurred headlights of another car coming at him in the opposite lane, and then it's past him and he's alone again. What had he told them about the fog? That it was beautiful, which it was, but you had to do an awful lot of mental acrobatics to make it that way, to fix it in your mind as something other than car exhaust and ice crystals. *Amazing*, they say, or *incredible*, or they just want to lick his body all over.

The body he's created and then shared with all of them.

It's been two weeks since he's come to town and he's a bit disappointed in himself, disappointed in the town too, as he reaches the first traffic light and slows to a stop. But what was he expecting, some kind of revelation? He lets go of the steering wheel and pulls off his cap. The truck is finally warm enough that he can begin shedding layers. By the time he gets to the dump he's gloveless and coatless.

He's not alone, because someone else across the parking lot is poking at debris with a ski pole, collecting treasures. Edison pulls on his hat and gloves—it's the fingers that go first—and hurls trash into the nearest dumpster, calling up a terrific racket of metal and wood. The guy across the way doesn't seem to notice, or if he does notice, he doesn't care.

The men here are ugly. They don't know how to treat you.

When did he say that? It was at the very beginning, typed out to someone he never saw again, and the guy had replied, *I know how to treat you.*

He spins the truck in a big arc around the lot before moving to the exit. Someone is driving in as he drives out, a beat-up truck a lot like his, a driver who looks a lot like him too except for the color of his skin and maybe some of his secrets. They wave to each other as they pass, an open-hand gesture that seems so half-hearted that it's almost insulting.

His evening is just getting started. The drunk girl at the Big I is practically dancing on her stool. She's trying to convince the people around her that they should all head out to a strip club, but nobody seems interested. The men watch the TV, smoke their cigarettes, and drink their drinks. Maybe they're a little defeated by the weather, maybe by her crazy energy, but mostly they just seem content. The girl has one foot on a chair, thigh spread open, and Edison takes note of the holes in her jeans, the bruises on her knees. If her hair wasn't so long she'd be a boy, and a starving one, with wild, crazy eyes. She says something about every single person in the place being a big pussy. Best to stay away, on the opposite end of the bar.

Edison orders a beer and the bartender says, "What have you been doing with yourself?"

"You know what I've been doing with myself," Edison says, because last month he made the mistake of mentioning the horse. He kicks his boots against the bar to clean off the snow, glances up at the TV in the corner. The drunk girl, she's moving down the length of the bar, spinning the empty stools, and as he glances at her face he realizes that he forgot to log off at home. His name, the name of the *fake* girl, is floating on the screen collecting messages. He fights the urge to slide off the stool and walk out. Instead he looks down at the burnished wood of the bar and tries to remember its story, the things the bartender told him. It had been driven up from the lower forty-eight on a flatbed truck, and it's classier than the place deserves, ornamented with little birds and so smooth he places his palm on it just for the sheer pleasure of the surface.

She says, "Are you in the military?" but she's talking to the red-headed kid next to him. They're the only two people in the place under thirty and now they've found each other. Except that the kid doesn't seem that interested, and she ricochets off him and over to Edison. "Take off your coat and stay a while," she says, and he realizes, yes, he's still wearing his coat, his black hoodie pulled up Unabomber-style. The bartender moves away, down to the safe end of the bar. "Black men," she says. "Black men."

Edison laughs like it's a joke. He wants it to be some kind of joke.

Certain men on his computer say they're black, but he guesses that they are not, that they're wearing that disguise just like he's wearing his. They meet there in the Neverland between computers and exchange their words and then they fuck him with their thick black cocks. The clichés are a form of punishment, much more so than the tying of the wrists, the insults, the descriptions of urination. It's like the story of a little prince who wanders through the kingdom in disguise and finds his likeness in a dirty beggar boy. He looks into the face of the other and sees himself and he gives himself over to it, surrenders to it, by switching places, by letting that other one inside his life. When it happens he sometimes types, *oh my god you're so big*.

The drunk girl touches his thigh and says, "There's nothing you can do that can't be done. There's nothing you can sing that can't be sung."

He ends up buying her a meal of fries and two cheeseburgers and he leaves before the food arrives. He decides it's stupid to drive the hour into Fairbanks and not do grocery shopping, so he heads to the 24-hour Safeway and walks up and down the aisles, collecting whatever catches his eye. It's three in the morning and by the time he's filled the cart he's lost in a woozy euphoria. The girl at the checkout is the opposite of the girl at the bar. She's smart and sulky, with short black hair and a mumbled, "How are you tonight?" A nose ring, of course, and about eighty extra pounds. She wears it all like a suit of armor.

The girl back home, the one he's created, is like neither of these people. In a way she's a solution to the problem posed by these people: more wholesome but with their brittle toughness, and when she spreads her legs she never surrenders completely. There is always something held back, that part of himself he shares with the real world, with the grocery clerk, the bartender, the man who sold him the sick horse. It's fun to think of himself as the secret she keeps, the thing that can't be shared.

Imagine me with my ass in the air. Imagine me dressed in my winter coat and nothing else. Imagine me.

Her skin is scrubbed clean every day, her experience unblemished by tragedy or failure or even a dull job like this one, working late at night in a grocery store. She tells him, "You sure like cereal don't you mister?" and eyes his groceries on the belt like none of his choices are right.

When he gets home he finds messages from fifteen different men, a perfect cross section of the lonely. Some of them he knows and others are first timers. Some misspell practically every word and others are meticulous in their punctuation. To each of them he has that remote, exotic thing, the thing they are trying to catch. *Alaska girl?* Shyboy asks, *where are you?*

He types, *I'm here.*

The coronet is disintegrating into yellow pulp, but he gets only a glance before the horse pulls back, turns sideways, drives its hindquarters into the damaged wall. It's a relief to see it cave completely, because now he'll be *forced* to repair it, but the horse is the more immediate concern. Its eyes have turned to white and it's making noise like a sputtering engine, and he has to crawl beneath it and push up, hard as he can, before it even moves an inch. He considers its weight collapsing down on him, and he considers the temperature, and then he pushes hard, from his knees, and the horse lurches sideways and there's nothing he can do, this is going to hurt. But no, somehow the horse finds its feet. He falls to the ground, right on his ass, and the horse sidesteps a couple of feet away, looks at him like he's some puzzling little creature. His tailbone hurts. So does his wrist. The wall is splintered outward. He wants to weep, but instead he dusts himself off and stands. His wrist is throbbing, although it's not bruised.

He wants to tell them, *I'm crying right now. I don't know why. Sometimes I cry during sex.*

His friend from the farm in Livengood calls and Edison tells him, "It's fine. I think she's doing better. She drinks plenty. That's a good sign, right?" And he tells Shyboy, *I don't like to drink but I like to dance. It's hard to find men around here who are good at dancing. All the clichés about Alaska men are true. The military guys just want to fuck you and the local guys don't even want that. They just want to fall asleep on top of you. But I love it here. I really do. Today I saw a raven I swear was the size of an eagle. It moved in low over my cabin and I thought it was going to land right on my stovepipe but it kept going.*

I want you to wear your tallest heels when you talk to me, Shyboy says. *Okay. Okay.*

The part about the raven is true, except that it happened last winter, and for some reason it had frightened him, like something beyond reason, bursting out from a dream, and remembering it now was like remembering a dream too: the incompleteness of it. That was when he was seeing that woman from Delta, briefly, and calling to mind her serious face made him feel like a weakling, the kind of man bothered by dreams. He had told himself that he would not allow her into his head anymore because she was not that important at all. He can't even remember her last name, but there she is, in his mind's eye, her neatly framed cabin and her big black stove and her on the porch, telling him things about himself.

Another message appears, asking for his age, sex, and location. *Black cock?* he types back, but the man doesn't respond, and he has to get back outside anyway and feed the chickens. But Shyboy writes, *You are the kind of person who everybody always thinks is doing fine.* Then they describe themselves in vivid language, one kneeling, the other pushing himself into her face. It's sort of boring and sort of exciting and he really should go outside. After all, it's two o'clock and in a half hour he'll have to spread the chicken feed around in the dark. The day can slide right on past you if you're not careful. *I love this*, he types.

He can't identify the source of his arousal. He's in her head, thinking about the raven and then thinking about the man's body, but he's also in *his* head, and the sex is a form of retribution. He feels sorry for her, he feels sorry for himself, but he also wants it to be as painful as possible. He types, *I've never, ever felt anything like this before*. It's December seventh, two weeks until the solstice and then everything will begin that slow spin backward toward the light. *I have to feed the dog*, he types.

I didn't know you had a dog, and then, *I think I'm falling in love with you.*

The horse begins refusing water in mid-December. Its stool is a healthy shade of brown, sweet smelling, but it pushes its head away when Edison tugs it down to the bowl. He keeps his hand pressed to the warm skin, waiting for a message to run from its body into his brain. This has become a performance that will measure him, and he's completely unprepared. He tells Shyboy an hour later, *my mother is dying.*

I'm sorry.

Shyboy's replies are slow, which means he's probably masturbating. Edison's mother is alive and well in Atlanta, strong and reasonably happy, and she calls all the time and hassles him to come to visit, complains about the stiffness in her fingers. But the words he types on the screen seem as true as anything he's ever said, and he reads them again, hanging there in the middle of all the filthy language. The reply comes eventually, and those words seem true too, as sincere as the words about spreading his legs, taking the thick cock inside. Outside it's snowing now, and the birch trees have lost their uniqueness, the way they do every winter by this time. It's hard to tell where one ends and the next begins, and it's so beautiful he has to pause in his typing to consider it as a discovery. The window is small and blue. It hangs like a mirror. He says, *The winter gets inside you here.*

Shyboy says he can't imagine what it's like. He says, *I would like to come to visit someday. We don't have to do anything. We could just go out for coffee. We could just kiss.*

My mother is the most important person in my life and she's dying.
Okay.
I just wish there was a way I could help but she's so far away.

A long pause, and for a moment he thinks the name on the screen is going to turn from red to blue and then vanish. That happens sometimes when Shyboy reaches his climax. He doesn't like to stick around. But no, an answer finally comes back, a few words at a time. *Sometimes I think you are lying to me.* And then, *Do you really live in Alaska?*

Yes, of course, he types. *I'm looking at it right outside.*

And when he goes out there he is surprised to find the horse standing a good twenty feet from the shed, almost at the tree line, head bowed, side covered with a spattering of hay. No miracle, because when he moves closer to it he notices the cut in its side where it pushed through the boards. It's breathing heavily, and as much as he tugs at its halter, it won't comply and go back inside. It doesn't take much for him to just give up and let it be. He ties it off to the fence with the rope and climbs into his truck, not bothering to let it idle before he spins out of the driveway.

The drunken girl is talking about her Thanksgiving, and the turkey she and her friends fried in a barrel. They stayed up all night eating and drinking and then slept the next day, and when she says this there's a light in her eyes like love. But where are those friends now? She's here alone again, drinking a rum and Coke, crunching the ice at the back her jaw. She tells Edison, "I remember you. I'm not hungry tonight. I don't need to eat this shit food. But thanks for that."

"Hey, no problem," he says.

"You have a beard now," she says. "It's curly."

"I had a beard before," he says. "I always have a beard."

The bartender doesn't escape this time. He stands right there, listening to them talk while he rubs down the bar. He says, "He does. He always has a beard," and he smirks as he pours a shot. It's thirty-five below out and people dance when they come inside, banging their snowy feet, shaking their mittened hands. Some of their cars are still running in the parking lot, waiting for them to have their fun. They'll run all night, or at least for a couple of hours while they order drinks.

"You have an accent," she says. "Where you from?"

"Georgia, originally. But that was a long time ago. I've been here longer than you've been alive."

"I'm twenty-seven."

"Well, I'm exaggerating then. I've been here eighteen years. I came up for some work and I just sort of stuck to the place."

He feels as if he's required to say something funny or out of the ordinary, anything but what he is saying, which is as mundane as a glass of water. But she seems interested. She's leaning into him, practically falling against him, and he's talking about the way it used to be in this town before it got all civilized in the early nineties.

"You can't imagine it," he says, and thinks about Shyboy. The thing is, the story doesn't make sense to him either, when he hears it aloud. He *liked* Atlanta, liked riding the buses with his teenage friends, a little gaggle of skin-and-bones boys with the same haircut, the same sneakers, the same slinky, overconfident way of walking. They'd ride in the C bus up to the courts on Plymouth Heights, talking bullshit at the back, and play basketball all day, slump against the wire fence in the heat and talk more shit. He doesn't tell the girl any of this, of course. It's all he can do to talk about working on the pipeline, and that seems like yesterday. "More money than I knew what to do with," he says. "It was obscene." He chooses this word carefully, but it doesn't register with her. She's laughing like he's told a joke, like he's boasting, but that's not it at all. He wants to be understood. There's a point to his story.

They find her car around back and climb inside. The cracked windshield is covered with fresh ice and there's something disconcerting about not being able to see ahead, but he stays put while she reaches across him to the glove compartment and pulls out a plastic bag. "I have some shrooms," she says, "but they'll hurt your stomach. I have some other stuff too." It's cold enough that the police won't bother them.

He knows what she's thinking, so he says, "I'm hung like a Jap," and immediately regrets it. At least she doesn't seem to be listening. She has her hands on his crotch but not gently. She seems ready to hurt him. Her jaw is set, her face as calm and unemotional as a soldier's. "Maybe we should do the shrooms," he says. He feels impossibly far away from everything. They might as well be a mile underground, or orbiting the earth in a satellite. He looks to one side and sees some headlights flash on, then off, and touches her hair and says, "I think you misunderstood something."

"I'm not a whore," she says, "but I do want to see the money."

"Then you definitely misunderstood." But he keeps touching her hair. His hand runs down her face, her skin so pale, and he tries to cast it in his memory as something indelible, like a feature of the landscape he sees every day. He tells her, "You need to change your antifreeze," because the vents are still blasting cold air against his feet. But she takes that as a joke too. She laughs like he's hilarious, and then she pulls a little switch inside herself and stops.

I met someone tonight, he tells Shyboy when he gets home.

A long pause that could mean one of a hundred things. *Interesting*, comes the reply.

A really nice guy, he types. *He's got a swimmer's body. Long crazy hair. He works for Fish and Game and we just sort of hit it off.*

Did you fuck him?

No. I like him too much.

He's inventing her, word by word. He's saving her from some strange place. But he has to go there to do it. He types, *I'm going skiing tomorrow. The snow is perfect for it. I like to go with my dogs.*

Sometimes you have two dogs and sometimes you have one.

They begin to describe their lovemaking, but this time there are no props. Shyboy simply gives him a dense description of a kiss, the soft coming together of the lips, the romantic tilting of a head. It's a beautiful description, actually, despite the couple of misspellings, and Edison can practically feel it. *I don't deserve that*, he types. *I've been horrible to you.*

You haven't. You're gorgeous.

Would I be a horrible person if I wasn't gorgeous?

You couldn't be horrible if you tried.

He thinks of the woman from Delta again, looking for clues in shifting memories of their breakup, but there's really nothing there to see. Maybe just a signpost driving him further back, to the other woman in Atlanta and the stupid things he said to her, but that could just be a false trail too. He types, *I have never lied to you ever*, and damn it, it's true, it's true.

Another description of a long kiss. The way the eyes close and the sound of the mouths coming apart. He's getting good at this.

Stuff the ball gag in my mouth, Edison types, but Shyboy won't give him that. All he gives him is a third kiss, then another, then another, each described in dreamy language. Edison types, *I have to go to sleep.*

Wait, Shyboy types.

The outside world is blasted white. He wades through it to the firewood stacked between two trees and begins to split. The cold makes it easy, and the logs crack and fly, one becoming two. He leaves them on the ground until he has twenty, twenty-five pieces, and then does the difficult gathering work. His back hurts to stoop. The fire takes its time getting started, but soon it's blazing, and he throws in scraps of bark, a cereal box, and watches them burn. The box collapses in on itself in a kind of beautiful surrender.

Four days until the darkest day of the year. Everything is still as if it were arranged in careful precision, the seven chickens huddled in their coop, the three goats gathered by the exhaust vent at the back of the cabin.

The horse's body is a kind of stove too, a hot thing drawing him in. It still won't go inside. In fact, it's walked farther away toward the edge of his property, but it lets him put his head against its side and then he is stroking its black marbled face and it's leaning to him the way it did with the wall but more gently. It seems to know the proper arrangement so as not to do him harm. He pushes back, as if into a hard wind, and he knows the wet eyes are unseeing as stones. There is some frenzied crazy place deep inside it where the heat originates. He pushes his face to it. Tuesday, Wednesday, Thursday, and then the solstice and the days run the other way. It's a kind of journey, toward that strange place, then the arrival, finally the trip home.

I want to tell you my real name, he says to Shyboy on Wednesday.
You don't have to do that.
But he says that he *does* have to, sort of, but the name that comes out is Sandra. *You are probably a lie*, Shyboy says, *but I don't care. I want to know you.* Edison talks about what he wants to do with his life, the adventures he wants to go on to Greece and Italy, her older brother stationed in Iraq. *I disagree with the war but I respect his decision*, he types. It's fun to give Shyboy what he wants, but not exactly. It's an act of kindness and it's an act of revenge and even when Shyboy goes silent Edison keeps talking. He hasn't talked this much in years. *I'm sorry if I feel a little damaged. I know what I blame it on. It was an ex-boyfriend. He treated me really poorly. I never could trust people after that.*

Liar, Shyboy types, and Edison thinks of the Delta woman again, the way she bit her thumbnail when she told him he was a difficult person to be around.

You're right. It's not that. I want it to be that but it's not.
I was just teasing.
Now you're the one who's lying.
I'm trying to tell the truth.
Me too. This feels like the truth.
I know.

I just wanted to rescue her, he types, and he pushes himself back from the keyboard, considers his words, moves in close. *Or at least I thought I did.*

They begin to kiss, or at least their doppelgängers do, and when the ball gag goes in and the straps go on it's a relief. This time it's described slowly and tenderly, as if he's making a present of her body. Then he splits her in two with descriptions of casual violence. Edison is outside it all, looking in, and inside it all, looking out, and the thought occurs to him that maybe it's he who needs to be rescued. The fantasy shifts on the axis of this particular thought, and in his head he creates a third person, a handsome man, a good man, who enters and stops the ritual, removes him from the rack and says everything is going to be okay. In this scenario Edison is both the body wrapped tightly and the man freeing the body, lifting it in his arms. Shyboy is the abuser. It's not difficult to think of him that way. *Are you enjoying yourself?* the villain asks, and when Edison doesn't reply, the name on the screen disappears.

"Admit you made a mistake," the bartender tells him that night. "That's all you have to do. You can borrow my gun."

"Where's that girl tonight?" Edison asks.

"Nora?" the bartender says. "Who knows. She might be across the street. She might be at the Midnight Mine." He arranges a plate for him, silverware wrapped in a paper napkin, a bottle of ketchup. He switches out his empty glass for a fresh one with a quick shuffle.

There's something comforting about watching a good bartender do his job. "She's a funny one," Edison says.

"Meth addicts usually are."

"She'll be okay," Edison says. "I have a feeling," and he considers her in that dark car, looking at the windshield like she can actually see something. She's talking, rambling, and he can't figure out what the point is, even now, remembering it. What is she telling him? She's telling him her life story, what has happened and what will happen. It's enough to make him believe. She's going to get out of this town and go to school in Florida where her sister lives and she's never going to step foot in this city again. "I have a Remington," Edison says, and the bartender nods.

So on Friday he takes the gun from the back of the closet and loads it and walks out to the shed with it pointed at the ground. He does not know how he will turn this into something that makes sense, when he floats in the ether with Shyboy, in that place where everything is just a story, but that doesn't matter so much at the moment. It's a beautiful afternoon, with the sun red and squat on the horizon, a new dusting of snow covering the landscape. The horse has moved a little closer and is waiting.

He's not the person raising the gun at the heavy skull. He's the person in the car, telling that sad meth addict girl that everything is going to be okay. Florida is a beautiful state, especially farther south, and he can tell she's smart as hell. He pulls back the bolt and sets himself and it's easy not to see the horse as anything but a target. It's a form of liberation, he decides, or at least an act of compassion, but when he pulls the trigger he's not even there, and all of it is *already* a story before the horse's dead weight hits the ground. His mother has passed and everything is so sad and there are so many things she never had a chance to tell her. But what comes out, hours later, is different. The words are like small accidents, but there they are, on the screen, and he can't take them back. The ball gag is back in his mouth but he's talking, rambling. *You're right. I haven't been completely truthful to you.*

I know but I still love you.

I'm not what you think.

It's okay.

He pushes something forward in his head, an idea of himself he's partitioned off, and he types, *I bought a horse. A sick horse. I was trying to save it, or maybe I just wanted to be with it when it died.* He types another sentence, a description of the horse, but he taps backspace and erases it, replaces it with a better lie. *And she's doing good. I think I did it. She's getting stronger. She's drinking lots of water. I'm going to ride her once the damned winter turns the corner.*

I've never seen a horse. You know, except for on TV.

Beautiful animals.

I'm sure they are, and you with her, riding her. That's beautiful.

But I'm not what I seem.

I know and I don't care. It's fine. I know who you are.

Maybe I'm some crazy drug addict. Maybe I'm going nowhere.

Edison forces himself to recall the kick of the Remington and the way the horse settled to the ground, as if getting ready for sleep, and then the girl in the car, with her staring, sick eyes. He tries to think of everything at once, holding each separate weight as carefully as he can, and in his imagination they are all alive, pulsing deep inside him like his own stupid heart. And it's a gift he can share with this strange man, this villain, who knows him so well, better than anybody has ever known him before. *You should see her*, he types, *close up.*

Lynne Knight

A Brief History of Landscape Painting

An ancient Chinese emperor once called all
the artists to court, hoping one would create
the perfect landscape. For almost a year
they labored. Then one dawn they gathered
in the palace, unrolled their scrolls & waited.
A rustling of silks as the emperor pressed

his ear to tree or sky. Finally, he left the hall,
calling back, *Those birds all sang too sweetly
or too long.* That night he ordered the scrolls
burned in the courtyard. By dawn, when smoke
streamed like mist from a river, thousands
of birds lay dead. The groundskeepers ran

for their spades. But when they returned,
the yard was empty, save for music so sweet
those who heard it began to dance. No one
stopped to eat or sleep. By the next moon,
the music had spread through the countryside.
Farmers abandoned their plows to begin

their own dance. Seed held. Rivers halted.
Everything stilled like landscape, except the wild
figures, dancing & dancing, the old emperor
among them, silks & bones whirling out
beyond the material, leaving nothing but willows,
sky, quick strokes of birds past hearing.

Forbidden

They looked so long into each other
I sometimes had to look away

Or sometimes they'd be sitting side by side
& he'd put his hand in her long hair
& I'd watch it lift, fall,
lift, fall,
all the while he was talking & she had her hand
on his thigh, maybe, or at her throat,
where I imagined she would hold it
in the calm after coming

She was beautiful, thin & soft breasted
Their children had names that sounded like water
Sometimes she'd go out on the porch & call to them
& it would be like hearing water run clear
over rocks
Once he went out behind her & ran his hands
along her thighs, up to her breasts,
where they stopped
When the children came down from the woods
he stood there like that, talking to them
She leaned her head back on his shoulder

I know you are impatient to hear it did not last,
it was too perfect, I felt betrayed the day I heard
they had split up
But nothing like that happened
They went on as they always had
The children grew, the years began to tell,
& whenever I would see them I would feel
the same insistent heat

One day she came alone
when she knew my lover would be gone
This was early on, their youngest girl still a baby
I was pregnant with my own, just beginning to show
She spooned brown sugar in her tea, no cream
Her eyes were green like the sea after rain

I've decided to tell you something she said
You & no other because something in your face haunts me
I love someone else, someone impossible
He doesn't even live in this country
She laughed, a terrible laugh, but not like weeping
Then the baby started to fuss & we went into the room
where we'd laid her to sleep on a sea of green cushions
I'll feed her she said *I won't be long*
I waited, thinking she would come back & tell me
things women tell each other about the forbidden

But she never mentioned it again
We had more tea, the day went down in ash
over the sea, & over the years
I understood she was transforming her husband
into the one she longed for, her life
into another life, even the way she said his name,
even the way she watched me watch her

Claire Schwartz

for Mrs. Halachmi*

it's you on the other end saying, "come,
come," and i hear the tongue flapping
beneath your tongue like a bird
crushed in a child's hand. we come,

packed in the small
and orange hour. pounds,
ovaries, appetite. you are falling
away from yourself slowly. you will not go

all at one time. i fall in love with time.
when you pull back from our embrace,
your hair clings to my hair.

teacher, let me wear
your body through this life.

these days, an elsewhere
pulls you close.

how small and hinged these bones
how they prick and break
into a thousand stuttering wishes.

the night is a fire
shot through with darkness,
the truth, an enduring
machine; it plods on. i am

i whom you named for your name.
you take my hand, you whisper to me.
on your vanishing tongue, a name
we have no thing for

distance is the primal fact

all day i make myself small
and wait to come home to the only woman
i let close enough to hurt
when i retract from her touch.
at the dinner she has made for us i continue
not to eat, press words like *bungalow*
and *ethereal* against my cheek's soft meat,
consider writing a dictionary that
catalogs words according to the pleasures
they give my mouth. i say *listless*
sounds like the inability to catalog
and listen as the steak cools. i think
about making a record called *the stink*
of distance. i wear all my clothes to bed.
when she reaches for me, i make my body
into a fist. somewhere a womb
is opening to take me in. the origins are brutal
and full of liquid. six years ago, i am at mt. sinai,
a hospital where there are brochures and men
with certificates and hands that have been washed.
now the things inside of me are sterile. i crave the desert
lodged beneath my fingernails, the honest sun
that pulls back my skin. no, i don't resent moses
his golden calf. there are days
i light myself on fire just to worship something
glittering. all the light here has passed
through a chemical bath and the promise

of reason. i have yet to see a poet smuggle
rape kit into a stanza and make it sing.
my lover's body is a metronome. i
listen as sleep portions her breath
into something even, perfect.
once again, i am held
on the outside of time.

in the dream, it's not a doctor
but the blond and wispy social
worker. *say ahhhhh*, she directs me. i say
nothing, but stick my tongue out as she lays down
the depressor and then, carefully, a tiny
potted plant. *you're all set*, she says cheerfully,
as i think about how i once saw a man
slumped against the wall of a subway station
gagging while no one, especially me,
helped him. i think about how i am
especially me and gag. ask the rats about the difference
between desire and survival. the underground city
is a rabid brain. all day, i walk around with my tongue
out just so. my mouth's roof becomes moist
then wet then a torrential downpour. the potted plant
blooms. years pass in my mouth. seeds,
new plants, vines, flowers, mulch, rot.
my mouth is a jungle. outside, it is evening.
i am sitting on a stoop on 104th street,
my tongue aching under this whole and florid world.
the social worker walks out of a bakery with coffee
and two scones and i think she must have a lover
or an appetite. she stops to look at my tongue
overgrown with foliage. *you should have said, "ahhhhh."*
you should have said anything.

i wake, this terrible and once-again miracle
of morning. my lover is a still-warm imprint
on the left side of our bed. she is not yet on a plane

bulleting across the sky in all directions
not toward me. desire is an imprecise vector.
i find her in the kitchen. all across america
lovers are looking at their lovers' backs
and wondering what comes next. mine pours the coffee.
we watch the steam rise, then go to a place
from which it can never be called back

*The poem's title is from James Galvin's "Three Sonnets."

Ephraim Scott Sommers

Impossible Kiss

In the dry fountain at the center
of the Sunken Gardens on one foot,

a woman in a coat of living pigeons
holds her breath, and—hallelujah—

where always there is doubt,
I am not afraid to call this *belief*.

Soon, someone already ashamed says,
she will lift her arms

like a conductor,
and they'll scatter right off

of her. We'll be on our own
again. But think of them

together *this* second, Lover.
I know you, Lover,

a piece of something
about to unhold

but holding
while, everywhere, people say,

Look! The world's wings
are coming apart.

My Father Sings Dylan at Sixty-Two

The old chorale voice chants, *Where there has been tragedy,*
there will be laughter, and I don't know if my father at ten knows it yet,
nitpicking the ugly dumpsters behind the theater where his mother
pawns him off every Sunday, my father babysat by the same movie
screen over and over until his mother's last called or eighty-sixed
out of her bar, my father handing a half-eaten banana or last bite
of found hotdog to his little brother, my father shivering the curb,
having had enough of being headlocked by his drunken mother's
drunken boyfriend, my father's scabbed hand finding the knife
and burying it hilt deep in the boyfriend's ass, father hurdling
out of the apartment and never coming back, and now
at sixty-two clawing with me through a chicken carcass
and acting out the stabbing and laughing because he knows
our lives are the greatest of jokes, so why not laugh at them,
at all fathers acting absurd with turkey legs or bowls of noodles,
or chili dogs or anything foody, at our fathers slinging sandbag-
and-squid rigs into the ocean, flipping tri-tip or sizzling
pinch baskets of scallops or homemade jalapeño poppers
on the barbecue pit, my father with three teeth missing
behind his drum kit banging "Knockin' on Heaven's Door"
into the microphone, my father having lived through the army
and forty-four years on his back on a creeper under eighteen-wheelers,
forty-four years of cigarettes and six-days-a-week and invincible grease
under his fingertips and dive-bar live shows and tie-dye, having lived
through a heart attack on Christmas day, my father sings Dylan
like a mystic hymn, smokes the live mic like a Lucky Strike because he's lived
this long enough to quit drinking, and we, his children and everyone else
in the world he never laid a hand on, listen, tearing into racks
of his secret-seasoned spareribs, the old family riddle all over our faces.

Emily Vizzo

Lucky

I meant no disrespect to my body.
Sleepless, I made my way to the outdoor shower
hard rosebuds of insect bites rising. Vitamin
B, lavender oil, tea tree oil, Benadryl, nothing helped
& nothing made me less of a feast to the predawn
mosquitoes & fleas. Long ago I held a mesh bag
seething w/ ladybugs, my first sense of wealth,
all that luck at once, released on the backyard rosebush,
tiny black mouths & bright buttery wings
pinching aphids. I cannot drown beneath the waver
of an outdoor shower, rubber sandals sucking against
a concrete drain, but I can try. Next to me a little girl
showers w/ her mother, tramping a plastic horse
through the soap scum & fallen
hair nests. The tiny cello of her body, like mine,
is covered in itched welts, the shape of her life
singing all around her, sunlight crashing
into the manchineel, itching & scratching,
a beautiful sunburn, bee stings. I am stranded
from her joy, the torn bag revealing its red bugs, their
black mouths fastened to my body sores
w/ hunger, w/ attentive love,
call it what you want.

Jay Merill

Breaking Free

Doña Fernanda Salvatierra Martinez. Hunched by the window working her little finger in her ear to loosen wax and staring out at the mango tree. Anxious because she wasn't seeing light. Something was intervening. She saw an unnatural heaviness where the brightness should have been; heard the heavy ticking of the hallway clock. Looked down at her watch. Both of them said 10 a.m. What was happening? It was morning but the dark kept on deepening. I am Chaska, Fernanda's maid. I knew it was only a horde of birds in flight above Cajamarca that clouded the sky, but Fernanda fell to her knees in prayer to Our Lady of Sorrows.

Help us Our Lady. Show us the light of the world. Open up this first day for us. The day of sun.

I read the thoughts of Fernanda. She listened for the parrot's warning but the parrot was silent. He had not called out since daybreak. Fernanda slept at daybreak, snoring in her high featherbed. Only I was up. Cleaning ever cleaning. Now that she was awake she would want me to polish the brass of her bedposts to make them shine. She was afraid of the creep of darkness, wherever it occurred. There was no restful Sunday for me. I carried the water bucket outside to the courtyard as on any other day. Fernanda watched with a critical eye. If water slopped out over the rim of the bucket onto the mats, she would be displeased.

"Stop that, Señorita," she croaked.

I tipped the water into the drain. She saw it go with a jealous look. Fernanda could not bear to witness any loss.

Because the parrot would not look at her, it brought on her frowning. When nights were fair and the parrot edged along his perch, dipped his head, winked like the stars in the sky, called out to her with a sound like the quacking of a duck, she was all smiles for the joy of the world. You could see the gleam of her gold tooth. At this moment she could imagine only sadness. She thought of her husband dead these five years, her childless state, the nieces and nephews whose existence reminded her of this, the boils on the underside of her feet, her fast-dimming eyes.

"Chaska, fetch me the coffeepot," she screeched.

Coffee to reawaken her, as though the day could begin again.

Light flooded the sky now in Cajamarca, but even so Fernanda would not be happy. The meat I bought that morning contained too much fat, the change from the vegetable market was less than it should have been. She wrung her wrinkled hands until the veins stood out like purple thread, scratched at her itching left shoulder blade where she had a triangle of rash to which I used to apply anti-irritation creams each night before she slept. She increased pressure on the boils by stamping her right foot on the ground. This caused her unnecessary discomfort. Fernanda sent me back out into the busy streets to the marketplace, where I had to ask for more money at the onion stall. The parrot watched me go and made a squawking sound. As I left the shadow of Fernanda's house I saw how clear the day had become. The sun kissed my nose, my cheeks. I would be twelve years old in three days. I hoped for many presents, I hoped for a mobile phone.

I sensed the parrot did not like me. Pedro was his name, but I never said it in my mind when I looked at him. He always squinted when I walked past as if he wasn't pleased to see me. The door of his cage was kept open and he sat outside on his wooden perch where he liked to shuffle up and down. If he caught sight of me he stopped his shuffling and went inside. I have always treated him kindly, brought nuts and seeds, and filled his water jar when it was empty. I cleaned his cage in the early mornings before Fernanda woke. He very rarely spoke to me though he enjoyed squawking away to himself at all hours. I wondered what he was saying.

It was bright afternoon. The day of my birthday had arrived but nothing was any different. I got up at the usual time and cleaned, took Fernanda her coffeepot at nine. I would get presents from my family, but my brothers had not yet come. I looked for them down in the yard. The window was open because of the heat. When Fernanda rose from her bed, the parrot was full of talk. They clucked together like chickens, expressing their dislike of me in shared looks. I was sorry to be there. I hated that parrot and wished him dead. In my mind I pictured him lying on the floor of the cage with his scabby legs in the air. What would Doña Fernanda do about *that*? I felt in a bad mood and glared at both of them. When I fetched water for the laundry, my hand clenched the bucket so that water spilled.

Fernanda flew into a rage, and the parrot moved jerkily along his perch. His eyes were as glassy as marbles. They rolled around in fast motion, and he hung his head. Fernanda shrieked about the spillage and sent me for the mop.

Slooshing and squeezing till the floor was clear I then gave the mop a shake. I waved it up in the air, its head like a giant carnival puppet with the face of a ghost, meaning no face at all, and all the gray hair hanging round the top of the wooden pole where you'd expect a face to be. The parrot did not like what he saw. He flapped and screeched before rising from his perch with a spread of wings to take your breath away and flew out through the open window, no stopping. Tail feathers were the last we saw of him as he shot upward in the sky.

"Come back. Come!" cried Fernanda. "My little Pedro, come back to me."

The breath was all but gone from my body in the shock of this moment, my throat dry as unwatered grass. Fernanda, too woebegone to scold me, was looking outward, looking, looking, her hand shading her eyes from the sun to see more clearly. Her precious Pedro had flown up into the mango tree. My breath slowly came back and turned to inward laughter. There was the parrot sitting stiffly on a midway branch. His green was brighter, lighter, than the leaves of the tree, his outline sharply visible. But Fernanda could barely see him. Her eyes were dim.

"He is resting in the mango tree," I told her.

She grunted but said nothing. Later the scolding would begin.

My brothers came in the evening and gave me a bracelet. It was gold colored but plastic on the inside. I tried it with my teeth. It was not metal, and the small hanging stones were pink and blue chips of colored glass. Our family meant to be kind, but they were poor. The bracelet would please a five-year-old. I thanked them, and they quickly left because they saw the frown lines between the eyes of Fernanda, smelled the venom waiting to burst out from under her skin. As they went they called to the parrot, telling the bird to go quickly back to his perch. Their voices had a sweet tone of encouragement, but I knew it would do no good.

At night I listened to the rising and falling murmurs of Fernanda, her supplications to Our Lady crackly with emotion. I lay on my mat by her door and waited for the snoring to start. How wicked I had been to wish for the death of the parrot. My punishment was to hear the pleas of Fernanda in vain. Night wore on. Neither of us slept. In the morning Fernanda rose early, hobbled out into the courtyard. I saw her peering up into the mango tree.

And the following morning the parrot still sat unmoving on his branch. We went out to him, Fernanda and I, calling together in clear voices. But he made no sign that he had heard. He stared into the hazy distance.

"Look," Doña Fernanda said. 'We have fine foods for you. Dear Pedro, we have the finest. Come down to us. We cannot reach the high-up branches where you are." Her voice was a sob. Yet still he did not listen.

"We have the sweetest nuts and seeds for you," Fernanda cried like a seller in the marketplace. But the parrot would not look at us.

Next day Fernanda went to the mango tree alone. I watched her through the window blind. Her dry, curled body was beseeching.

"Dearest Pedro, I wish for you to come. Our home is waiting for your presence." Again I heard her tears.

On the fourth and fifth days Fernanda and I went to him early. We offered his favorite seeds. I said nothing but Fernanda spoke in a voice of tender whispers. The parrot stared out above our heads with hardly a blink.

"Come," Fernanda coaxed, but he made no response.

I felt tearful and wondered what would happen. I blamed myself. Surely the parrot would wither and die. He had eaten nothing. How could he continue to refuse the food?

For one week it went on, this nightmare. Each day Fernanda hobbled to the mango tree. Sometimes I was with her, sometimes I watched from the window. She stayed out in the courtyard till the sun was high in the sky, her hands outstretched with offerings that the parrot would not take. Then came Saturday.

It was morning. I woke on my mat outside the door of Fernanda. The sky was radiant with sun. I took in the coffee jug to my mistress, and the early morning breakfast tray. But I saw how her heart was set hard against me and it burned my soul. I felt I had done wrong and she had somehow been a witness. It made me hang my head to think how I could not help hating the parrot. His disobedience was my trial. I wished I could be through it, that there was somewhere to go that did not spell out misery. He must eat soon. Even *I* prayed for this to happen. Fernanda had fallen asleep, the coffee untasted. I knew she had been awake all the night through. I took away the coffee jug and went about my daily chores. Glancing through the window I saw the outline of the parrot in the mango tree. I had the feeling he was one branch higher than he was yesterday but couldn't say for sure. I put on my fake gold bracelet, regretting the lightness of its weight against my arm. Outside, the sun rose yet higher in the sky, and then suddenly the world became dim.

And Fernanda had woken. I heard her voice through the wall very scratchy, calling to la Virgen de los Dolores to save the parrot, praying for her intercession as darkness loomed. Looking through the window I saw dense green waves pulsating overhead, as though sea had flooded out the sky. And a terrible screeching had risen up, so that I was full of fear. Then I understood it was a host of parrots bound for the southern Andes. I remained at the window waiting for the tide of moving birds to pass. At last the sun returned, the sky was blue again, and quiet descended. And the parrot was no longer in the mango tree. I went out and searched for him on every branch, but he was nowhere.

Doña Fernanda Salvatierra Martinez as a small child was very happy and her young days were filled with laughter. Fernanda told me that only the parrot had reawakened this joy in her. Now he was gone. She lay still on her bed facing toward the wall. She was silent, like stone.

Doña Fernanda sent for my brother to fetch me after Pedro flew away. She blamed me and would no longer keep me in her house, she said. I cried at first and did not know what would become of me, as there was no room at our place. Also I did not like the broken tap where the rats came to drink at night, and I asked myself if that was why my father didn't stay. But my mother told me I'd be going to Lima, and my aunt would take me into her home. I felt glad about this. I would learn better Spanish and go to a good school. There was plenty of work and also I must help Aunt, Mother said. I did not mind and felt very excited about it all. They say my father is in Lima too, and I wondered if I would meet him there.

In one week my aunt came to fetch me. She took me away on a bus. We drove through the night and all the next day. I was sick and then I slept and then I was sick and slept again. My head felt heavy with the droning of the bus, and when it swerved around sharp bends I got a headache and couldn't look out the windows for fear of seeing the steepness of the road. Sometimes the bus seemed to take up the whole space and Aunt worried that something would come from the other way and we'd crash or be tipped over into the valley. She clung to the bar of the seat in front and bit her lip. All the time she kept muttering, and this was worse than the sound of the bus itself. I wished I could sleep for the whole journey and wake up when we got to Lima. But my stomach hurt and every so often Aunt screamed out when we wobbled fast around a corner. And she wasn't the only one. Plenty screamed at each corner, and then the driver swore and shouted. I hid my eyes and hoped that if we were all to die it would happen quickly. But when we arrived at Lima Bus Station, my fears were at once forgotten. All were smiling. I smiled too, as I felt very happy that I had come to this place. I was seeing the world, and I would learn Spanish. I'd get a very big job and be rich. I was too tired to sing as I stumbled along the Lima street with Aunt, my heavy bag over my shoulder, but I would sing the next morning. I knew this.

But things at Aunt's were not so good. Sometimes she was crosser than Doña Fernanda. There was also the husband. I tried to think of him as Uncle but I did not like his eyes and the way they squinted sideways at me when he pretended to be looking elsewhere. He made a squirting shape with his mouth when I walked by him and I imagined water in a spiral coming out from between his lips. I thought of an elephant I once saw in a movie. But this uncle was not so friendly as I think an elephant would be. In the aunt and uncle there was an equal hardness. At nights I had to sleep on a cushion on the floor at the bottom of their bed. Miri, Silvana, and Juan Carlos shared a big bed next to the window. These were my cousins. Before this I had hardly ever met them. They blinked their eyes sleepily at me when I came into the bedroom and then they were lost to the world again. I lay on the floor cushion and dreamed of softer times.

I had been at school each morning for a week. Aunt took me there the first time. The other children stared at me when I spoke, and I saw sneaky laughter tumble out from the corners of their mouths. Sometimes they put their hands over their lips, but it was in such a way as to show me they were laughing. A boy I did not like at all asked me why I spoke Quechua. They all laughed openly then, and I did not know what to say. A girl I didn't like asked me why I tied my hair up at the back in a ribbon. I had no idea what to reply to this either. Aunt said I had to start to work and help the family if I knew what was good for me. She told me I must come out of school until next year. Most likely Aunt thought I was unhappy about this, but in reality I was happy because my prayers had worked and Madre Dolorosa still remembered me and was not angry that I had gone away.

My aunt said I must walk at night near the cinemas and bars in Miraflores. I was not used to being alone in the dark of a city, and I felt smaller than I ever had since reaching twelve years old. She told me I would be selling packets of sweets as she used to do before she had too much work to see to at home. And she showed me how to go up to tourists and ask them if they wished to buy *los caramelos* and how to take the money. I had to carry a large bag with the candy inside and when it was empty I could come home and she would stock me up again. Even if I felt hungry at times I must never eat the contents, she was careful to impress on me. Uncle stood next to Aunt when I left the house with the bag next evening.

"Do not eat the sweets," said Aunt, "or it will be the worse for you." She told me to keep out of the way of the police or they would take away my stock. Uncle was already drunk and wobbled sideways as Aunt spoke. He said nothing but looked at me with dangerous eyes. I felt frightened and wished I had not come to this place of hardness.

As I stood with my little bags of candy one late evening feeling very lonely, this girl a little older than I was came over and talked to me. She was a hot dresser and held a great new shiny phone. Her name was Pilar. She was fourteen and she had many friends. We went to a stall together and she bought me a Pepsi. I gave her some of the *caramelos* and I had some too, and I told Pilar then that I was afraid to go home because we'd eaten the sweets. A night earlier in the week, when I couldn't seem to get any buyers, I had gone home with very little money and Aunt had shoved me in the chest. She said I must never come without money ever again or there would be mega trouble. Pilar only laughed. Her laughter had a tinkly sound that was pleasing to hear. She told me she was my friend and she would take me to meet some of her other friends, that she would let them know I was kind and I had given her sweets.

We went to a deserted building. I did not know how we got there and was sure I wouldn't remember how to get back.

"Do not worry," Pilar said, and so I tried not to.

Outside, the building looked derelict, and it was boarded up at the lower windows; inside, as we went in, there was some rubble. But upstairs it was spacious and oldie-world, and a fine staircase broken only in a few places had led to the higher level. Even the oldie-world carpet was still intact, red showing through the layers of dust. Pilar told me the place was once a cinema. She said her brother was in charge and he had a broken finger from when he'd had a run-in with the police. About thirty kids were sitting around in a large high-ceilinged room and Pilar said, "Hi, this is Chaska." A few came forward to talk to me. When Pilar told them I was afraid to go home because we had eaten the sweets, they said I could stay if I wanted, but I thought I ought to go because if I stayed away all night Aunt would be even more angry.

Dario, the older brother of Pilar, handed me some money to give to Aunt so she would think I'd sold the sweets, ". . . to the turkey-tourists," Dario said. Some kids asked me why the tourists were like turkeys, and then they explained it was because turkeys are too full of stuffing to fly. If they fell in the water they would sink. Everyone laughed at this great joke. Dario counted out the coins for me with his broken finger. Raul, the friend of Dario, wanted to know how old I was and if I had ever tried to sniff some glue. Dario and Raul had shaved heads; they were cool kids. Then Pilar showed me the way to go home and I was glad about this, as I felt a bit nervous in the company of so many street children. It was all very different from what I'd been used to.

Unhappily, it got worse at Aunt's by the day. I could not think of it as a home; they did not want me there. Aunt said I was just an extra mouth to feed and barely spoke to me, though she sometimes shouted very loudly, which hurt my ears because she always stood so close. If I did not sell all the sweets in my bag, she sometimes slapped my arms until they burned. Now and then Uncle felt my legs with his hand when I passed him. Then my skin was cold with anger. The four cousins stared at me from hollow eyes. They had no smiles for me. I was happy when I left the flat and went to work on the street. It was less scary and more comforting there. Pilar, my friend, often came to talk to me. She was usually high from sniffing glue, which she kept in a plastic bag under her sleeve. I was afraid of this but also I wanted to try. She showed me how to make my world serene; how to swim through its clear waters.

Soon it was the feast of The Lord of Miracles. Purple drapes hung from many windows. Great crowds of people walked on the streets. I knew their prayers:
Save us our Lord. Show us the path of true light.
I had special aniseed sweets to sell. Aunt was less severe because of the fiesta; the cousins were almost friendly. They all stood near me while I offered the *turrones* to passersby. These were a lot more expensive than the ordinary sweets. I saw inside the mind of Aunt. She counted up the money I was making.

Next minute there was a great throng of street children. Though they were many, one or two of them I recognized. There was the shaved head of Raul, there was Pilar in her flashy gear. A minute later I noticed Dario pass by wearing a leather hat. Looking out from the street corner where I was positioned I saw this dense stream of kids surge past like fast rushing water, or a shoal of bright fish. Quick as silver, they cut through the crowd, which seemed to part for them in panic. For a minute I remained where I was, and then I suddenly leaped forward and flung myself into the heart of the stream. It moved forever on and I moved too. I was a part of the wide flowing river. Then we were gone. The crowd reformed behind us, calm descended. Aunt and the cousins would search for me with their eyes along the pavement where I was standing but I was nowhere. Or nowhere they could ever know.

Michael Fulop

The Family

One summer two cellos fell in love.
And the next summer the lady cello
gave birth to a baby.
It was not a baby cello, however.

It was a violin with a high squeaky cry.
They fed it and they wrapped it in warm clothing.
But it did not grow.
It played music, of course, but a squeaky music.

The cellos looked at each other in silence.
In recrimination.
And at night they slept
with their curved backs against each other.

My Daughter's Courage

My daughter was three years old.
A long car ride to our summer vacation.
And then we walked down to the ocean.
Already it was late afternoon.

She was halfway in size between me and a seagull.
She looked at the waves.
She looked at the churning greenish water.
I want to go in the deep end, she said.

A Summer Storm

In the hot afternoon it came on quickly.
The sky almost black. Hail began falling.
In the long grass of June
the hail looked like white eggs.

It was almost the summer solstice.
A steady hail out of the dark sky.
And then it stopped.
The sky brightened with a peculiar orange color.
Like a sunrise in milk.

The birds were confused and seemed to think
it was dawn again and began speaking loudly.
And to me too it felt like dawn.
But the red sun was descending.

Joannie Stangeland

Poem to Chibok, Nigeria

#bringbackourgirls

I think of you as I stir the sauce—garlic,
oil, tomatoes I pressed through the mill—
imagine the spoons your daughters grip
in strange rooms. Dear mothers, daily
I ask for your daughters' return to you, *safely*.
When the men said *married off*,
I added *to their original families*.
How careful we must be in our prayers.

I think of your daughters stirring at fire pits
or stoves, open doorways framing the noon
that leads nowhere, the air itself a prison,
young women stirring words in their heads.
I think of the words in your hearts,
the words you shout in the streets.
God bless your shouting.

A mother is a mother all her life.
All daughters are our daughters.
We feel the space in our bodies
where they lived, we feel the echo
of their skin against our palms
when we held hands crossing the street.
Our hands miss their hands.

Dear mothers, I think of your grief in this absence,
your sorrow when they talked about truce,
the bitter flavor those lies left. What is a family
ripped apart? Empty, the way the pot is empty,
after it is washed and dried.

Prodigal

The house exhales behind me,
        drains its rooms of resting air.
                The physics of leaving
echoes in my kitchen cupboards

as though my heart's four chambers
        emptied in one beat.
                The theater of waiting.
Maybe the curtains fidget.

The daughter arrives in town
        minutes after I must exit
                for a desk at the office complex.
And thus the house sighs.

By my day's end,
        the stop-start-stop home,
                she will have left with friends.
The physics of drama.

Light chases the shadow's face
        and the cat follows the sun on the rug.
                The door asks and asks
an open-ended question.

Karen Craigo

The Houses We See from the Highway

There's a thing your fingers remember:
flocked wallpaper of an empty house,
and how you rested your hand and believed
its walls overtaken by moss. Such luxury
for a house abandoned, no chair or table
upright, no book or dish remaining to tell
its story. You've always wondered
how houses are quit, imagine families
standing, pushing back from the table
one last time. You'd enter them
when you were young, and always
you were tentative, leaning in
from the threshold, half expecting
a shout through a glassless window.

Paul Martin

The Radish

Just the two of us and a gray old guy
behind the bar in the country hotel
my brother and I found after swimming
that afternoon in a quarry.
No television, no music from the jukebox,
we sat in the quiet of polished wood,
sunlit silver keys hanging from a chain,
a faded plastic rose beside the brass cash register.
So many years later, my brother gone,
the hotel razed to a weed-overgrown space,
I tell you, as we pass, about the summer day
we stopped here for a cold beer,
how, as the three of us drank in the stillness,
the humblest things were lifted
into the light, how I felt such closeness
toward my brother and the old man
slicing an icicle radish
he took from the cooler, salting it,
and offering, as a gift,
the crisp white rounds on a plate.

Ghost

Especially when I wake early
on a spring morning and drive the back roads
to Baltimore, my pale, lost brother appears
in the passenger seat, staring
at the perfectly kept Amish farms,
the huge draft horses pulling a plow.

One word aloud from me would hurry
his leaving, so we drive in silence
past the remembered villages and river.

At what moment he slips away
or for what reason, I don't know,
only how longingly
he stares at the green fields,
the dirt lanes leading to white houses,
the lines of freshly washed clothes.

Julie Henson

Diplomatic Efforts, Ouija Board

for my sisters

Our séance for Henry Clay, noted diplomat.
Clever about it, we keep our hands just right, start, *hello,
can you confirm your identity okay please*

teach us treaties, teach us to get along with our stepmother. It's slow
    going. She walks barefoot
in drainage ditches near Belle Union, naked, tweaked out of her mind.
She offers to sell us the ashes, the heirlooms.

I add an impression of her Indiana accent, *ode* instead of *old*, *code*
    instead of *cold*.
The Colombian doctor did not understand when she said, *They're always
    so code,*
referring to my father's hands after treatment.

"Stop talking trash to ghosts," my oldest sister says. "That's not the
    point."

We dare not summon our father, who is sure to be biased.

Earlier I found a leaf bug on a chain-link fence across
from the Coca-Cola distribution center.
My other sister was inside watching *Hoarders*, eating cottage cheese &
    pineapples,
spooning mounds onto round crackers. *Have you ever met someone and
    just known*

they were trouble? she said. I couldn't answer.
I went back outside to the leaf bug, which—*God!*—did look like a leaf.

When overwhelmed, it flattens out, *stiff as a board,*
light as a feather, like my father's name now he's dead.

Henry, they call you both War Hawk & the Great Pacificator, such a
    blighting dove.
At the funeral, my stepmother straightened
her collar, said *it's my day.*

Is this what it looks like to bargain? Take the living, go ahead, why don't
you let her take them. Take the whole 8th floor of the VA,
each tightly made bed. Televisions mounted, tuned to *A&E, Dynasty of*
    Whatever.

In the middle of a curve there's no pulling out. So Henry, we go on,
    wanting
nothing now. Like an empty bowl, a door off its hinges.

And the Abyss

Every love story is a ghost story.
DAVID FOSTER WALLACE

Always the same deal, *return to sender.*
                Ghosts, lovers, the mail. My new mantra, *Heaven*
will protect the working girl. Not from erosion,
      the side of a hill that grows steeper or less steep,
Any particular heartbreak. Instead: existential. Dante's inferno,
    Angels and Not Angels, la de da.
Look into the abyss and the abyss will look back at you, Nietzsche says.
        Come bride take my name, the radio sings.

Benji tells an urban legend: phantom motorcycle driver looking for his
   OneTrueLove.
     Out on the bridge past midnight
in Okeanna, Ohio, flash your brights,
            he'll come to the car. When they tried it, Benji got the willies
so bad he saw orange, almost passed out.
        At First Beach in Washington, the Pacific threw an entire driftwood
   tree
     onto shore. Once, after a date,
every streetlight
    I drove under turned off with a wink.
       My thought: something sinister playing itself out.
Like houses at dusk, low-flying planes, like an empty closet.
    In New York City,
             a strange boy got in bed with X and would not get out.
I don't let myself think about
    the things I can't think about.
          My sister balances on two logs at a driftwood beach
and it is easy to believe she will not fall.
       The wind howls on Mount Moscow, Bethany says, so forlorn.
   For no reason, you'll find peaches rotting
        near the entrance to the most winding trail.
The stoplights in my town tonight are all red, hyperbolic,
   stop stop would you just stop. So I do.

Bernard Matambo

In the Name of the Tongue

Come Sunday afternoon and I sat back hunched
in the car, thumbing my father's Bible, the door slamming

behind him, as though his gun had burst a nest of birds.
I fingered the grime into my hair and sat rehearsing,

Thou shalt not steal, Thou shalt not bear false witness
Thou shalt not covet thy neighbor's house,

my father's sweet-tongued weights turning coolly on my tongue
as I thought again of that verse in which the woman

wets Jesus' feet with her tears and mops them away with her hair,
the lean long day sliding past, hot in the nest of my jaw.

It was always the same house we stopped at, Baba and I,
the one whose eaves hung low like the milkman's sly eyes

when they followed Florence Wida's behind
and made him clang his bell more slowly.

Afterward Mami's anger rose when she caught
the jasmine and talc tight on his neck

like a noose. Something must have burst holy out of her
those nights, all night her tongue flailing,

fire coming down through the walls louder
than when they made love and he whimpered afterward.

How I reached into the darkness and tongued
the contours of his sins.

Thou shalt not steal, Thou shalt not bear false witness
Thou shalt not covet thy neighbor's house.

It was a sport I knew little of then
except for the beds in the corners of his eyes

when he returned delicate with his thunders.
He liked golf and always took me to the driving range

afterward, his hand in a glove, holding firm his stick.
Tomorrow, he said, you will learn how to drive.

The Last Time I Saw Annamore Tsonga

The last time I saw Annamore Tsonga was at the protest in Highfield, the one where people got beaten up and teargassed, and Gift got shot by the police and later died from excessive blood loss and gunshot wounds. The last time I saw Annamore she was a pile beneath heavy baton sticks and big shiny black boots that branded her body with a swathe of vulgar bruises. It was a Sunday, in Highfield, the last time I saw Annamore Tsonga. It was a prayer meeting. Her lips were heavy with curdled blood. She could barely walk and her face was fat with wounds that suffocated the warm charm of her cheekbones. Later, I could not find her face in the morgue, days after Gift Tandare's funeral, where the police took Gift's body away because too many people wanted to bury him, to celebrate his life, and to weep for Zimbabwe. Something about it all reminded me of those scenes on television about apartheid South Africa: mothers crying after their shot babies, bludgeoned sons in police cage trucks, bludgeoned daughters in blood. How far, we thought then, we were from it all.

Sarah Giragosian

Easter Dinner

First, there's the prayer over the roast;
both are tidy, greased with devotion.
God is at the table. Some wife is too,
and an overhandled infant girl,
who tries and tries to squirm out of reach
but is always brought back to eat.
He sharpens his knives and carves the bird.
Later his teeth grind down on politics and gristle.
He prefers his meat to be soft as an earlobe,
the wings and face avulsed from the body,
all traces of her life and death
dismembered from the table.

Someone could recall the bird before
when she nipped ice crystals out of her wings
and sunbathed at dawn. Or someone
might speak of how she sang her horror through blood
when they shackled her legs,
hung her upside down, and slit her throat,
cutting her head clean off. But no one does.

In time, he will leave the table
to colonize a TV chair and nod off,
and the wife, humming to herself,
will clear the carnage from the table.
The night will come, the Resurrection will pass,
and all of her life the infant with her overlarge eyes
will carry a hunger in her belly
for something else.

Kerry Cullen

Parts

The night before Lissie comes back, I am up late at the kitchen table, cramming for a biology test. I've been staring at the drawings for so long that the bodies don't make sense anymore when I hear wobbly clomping down the stairs.

Taylor clacks into the kitchen in her ivory satin pumps, her hair tied up in an elaborate bun, stray curls loose around her neck. She yanks the fridge door open and stares in, her face drained in the blue-white glow.

"You look insane," I inform her. She whips around, almost slipping on the tile. "What are you doing up?"

I hold up my textbook and make a face. She shakes her head, tromps to the sink, fills a glass with water.

"Well, I'm practicing." She takes a big gulp of water and twirls, almost slipping.

"You look like a poodle in stripper heels."

She stares at me, her eyes huge in the late-night kitchen, her cheeks puffed with water. And then she explodes, spitting water, her arms clenched over her stomach while she laughs, and she slides to the ground with her back against the fridge, slow and halting so she won't slip on the wet floor. She keeps laughing and I catch it too. I go over and sit with her, both of our shoulders shaking, neither of us able to speak.

"So, is Trevor walking around in his tux all the time too? Practicing?"

Her smile flickers. "Trevor's different."

"Like how he leaves?"

She shrugs. It's become a family joke—how when he's frustrated with Taylor, with anything, he just leaves: out of the room, out of the house, to who-knows-where. Sometimes for just a few minutes, sometimes for hours. When he comes back, he pretends nothing happened, and so does she, so we do too. "I just don't understand it," my mom sighed, once, when neither of them were in earshot. It's not the funny kind of joke.

"Yeah," Taylor says, reaching up and gripping the fridge door handle, ready to pull herself back up.

"Why?"

She lets go and slumps, sighing and pulling a loose thread from the cuff of her shirt. "I don't quite know, Jackson. Some people are afraid of themselves."

"No, I mean: why are you marrying him, then? He doesn't seem—" I look around the dark kitchen, hoping the right word will blink into frame. "Happy."

She is quiet, her eyes cast down. The faucet drips.

"Just because a story isn't happy all the time," she says, "doesn't mean that you don't want to hear it."

"That's a shitty reason."

She smiles quickly, like a spark about to catch. "It's being a person," she says. "It's hard."

I nod. I rub some of the water into the tile, spreading it across the floor in such a thin layer that it dries immediately, becoming nothing. She smiles closed-lipped and smoothes an errant curl behind my ear. "Your pretty hair," she says. "I spent two hours getting mine to curl. Why'd that have to be the one way we don't look alike?"

I shrug.

"Plus," she adds as if in afterthought, her eyes bright and tired, her own hair falling out of her bun, "it's not like he's the only important person I have in my life."

I look at her.

She smiles, winks, and points at me like a cheesy movie star would. "I've got you."

Today, I wake up thinking about weddings, Taylor's wedding in specific but also just wondering what it might be like to let another person see you whole. I stumble to the bathroom, already feeling the regret stir in my stomach. I hoisted the full-length mirror out of my room months ago to make these moments less convenient. But I can't turn off my eyes, and on some days, some twisted part of me wants to see.

I used to take scalding showers and only look in the mirror after, when the steam still blurred my body. I'd curve into shapes that would look ridiculous if I normally made them. I don't remember the exact moment when I started hating my body. It was sometime around when I started growing hair all over and everything else. Hulking around, eating about twice as much as Taylor eats, growing bigger than her, getting lankier and stronger whether I liked it or not. My voice grating lower, and lower, and it hasn't even settled yet. Every reflection is still a jolt. I don't look the way I imagine myself. I don't look the way I should.

I need to keep my image clear, gruesome as it might be, especially now. I need to keep in mind what Lissie will see when she looks at me. I go to Taylor's room and knock. When there is no answer, I crack open the door.

Everything here gleams, dappling the wall in light. A mobile of dewy sea-glass shapes hangs against her window. Sun filters through gauzy silver curtains and glosses over the pictures taped around the edges of her mirror—herself and her friends in jarring, wild makeup and poufy old dresses, playing Princess, or Prom, or Wedding. I can almost smell the clotty nail polish that used to seep out into the hallway during sleepovers, tinged with remover and eventually drowned in sticky gusts of Love Spell perfume. I take a gulping breath and close her door, so I can see myself in her full-length mirror.

My hair is wild, which is my only fixable problem. My head looks clunky against my neck, my arms both too bony and too thick. My lines jolt instead of easing. I look at myself and I don't make sense. I twist, seeing myself from the side—the slight dip of my sternum, the V of my hips. My body is too harsh, too big, and it gives me a sick rush of unfamiliarity whenever I see it. The closer I look, the more wrong it feels. A calm horror, an undeniable knowledge that this will never change and cannot be fixed. Just when I feel the most gutted, the screaming downstairs begins.

"Lissie!" Taylor squeals, happy, almost falling down the stairs. She slams her whole small body against the door to push it open.

"You walked? We could have picked you up!" She bursts out the front door in a froth of joy. The grown-up girl on the threshold with the army-green backpack and the leather bag over her arm looks unsure but then grins—and she's Lissie again, even with her lips painted dark red, her hair cut shorter, eyes lined purple. Silver chains and pendants loop around her neck and fall from her collarbones to the top of her ribs.

She wears a dark flannel shirt and a worn denim jacket. A rainbow wristband peeks out from one cuff. She's almost as skinny as Taylor, but where Taylor's body looks anorexic-chic, her veins sea-glass colors that show too well through her skin, her bones almost poking out, Lissie is opaque, tanned and freckled, and strong.

"It's not a bad walk from the train station." Lissie cracks her gum and grins. "I wanted to get used to this place again."

Taylor kicks off her heels, jumps off the porch steps, and hugs Lissie, grabs her hand and yanks her up the stairs to the house. "I have so much to tell you," she says, practically skipping with glee. "Come on! You have to see the dress in real life." I start following them up the stairs, but when Taylor notices, she gives me an inscrutable look.

Lissie catches her meaning, whatever it is, and smiles wryly at me, lifting her free hand in a small wave while she's pulled along. "Long time, Jackson," she says, "We'll all hang out later, yeah?" She trips on the bedroom threshold and falls inside, laughing. Her laugh is different than I remember it, lower now, and hoarse. "Yeah, long time," I say back, trying not to squeak, but the door is already slamming shut.

I was nine years old when Lissie left, the day after they water-tortured me. They couldn't find a way to keep me still against the ground, so they figured they could do it vertically, with their fingers. That way they didn't need water either.

They tied me to the crabapple tree in the backyard and blindfolded me with Lissie's hot-pink bandana. They set their watches to twenty minutes because "If we do it longer," Taylor said, "he could die." They approached me one by one and tapped their pointer fingers hard in a constant drumbeat, taking turns every twenty Mississippi seconds.

Lissie kept her hair up back then, tied in two flimsy blonde side-buns. She snapped her gum to punctuate her sentences and blew bubbles to draw out her pauses. The popped bubbles stuck to her nose and wilted against her shiny skin. I could tell between the two of them, even blindfolded, because my sister Taylor and I both bit our nails, and Lissie's mom manicured hers.

The sharp-filed points had been stabbing my forehead for longer than their usual turn when they stopped altogether. Her sticky whisper next to my ear: "Taylor's gone, Jackson."

Since now I only had one opponent, I debated kicking out in front of me. Lissie leaned in again, her breath cloying and sweet. "You know I'm moving away tomorrow, right?"

I nodded. Taylor had already thrown a couple of fits. She'd concocted a plan to kidnap Lissie and keep her in our tree fort until her parents gave up and stayed.

"All the way to California." She blew a bubble so big it touched my nose before it popped "I want to kiss a boy before I leave."

I tried to wipe my damp hands against the tree bark, but I couldn't wriggle the rope loose enough.

"I'm going to kiss you, Jackson," she whispered.

"Can I take off the blindfold?"

"No."

Her lips tasted like strawberry Bubblicious, and sort of felt like it too. I licked my mouth, tasting sugar.

"When can I take it off?"

"When you escape."

"What if I can't?"

"Don't tell," she said, eraser-burning my right arm for emphasis. Then, in a lift of weight and shadow, she was gone.

Now, after Lissie and Taylor have had their girl time and I've been graciously invited to join them, the three of us sit in a triangle at the base of that same tree where Lissie kissed me eight years ago. It's early afternoon, and autumn sunlight sifts through the branches. Lissie pulls individual strands of grass out of the ground and pries apart their threads with her sharp nails. The way she picks at things makes sense to me. I recognize it: I know she's trying to get at the pale roots, to yank the hidden tangles into view. I wonder what Taylor sees.

"Shouldn't we be gluing seed beads to something?" I ask, slumping back against the trunk. "Or flower arranging?" I shiver. My shirt is worn cotton that used to belong to someone else. It feels lighter than wind and sleek against my chest.

Lissie and Taylor are more prepared for autumn—layered tank tops and flannel under sweaters and scarves. Ribbed tights, scuffed boots. Lissie wears royal blue and ivory, plus her silver chains and a cloth hat with floral appliqués. Taylor dresses darker, more sparse and dramatic—cracked garnet lipstick, black knit scarf, flowing forest green skirt.

When I get dressed, I just put on whatever's clean, and it never feels right. I wonder how girls learn to do this. They look as if they fit into themselves; if you switched their clothes, they would each look out of place. Lissie would look washed out with dark lips. Taylor avoids white like the plague.

I met a guy once who was dressed like a girl. His lipstick was bright and his stubble poked through the caked-dry paint on his face. The cashier had given a double take. He'd tried to pretend that he wasn't freaked out, but he talked too fast and dumped the guy's change on the counter instead of placing it in his hand.

The guy was very polite. He peered down from his stiletto-heeled height at the cashier, thanked him in a low, even voice, and tottered off into the night.

I stood numb in the romantic comedy section, watching. The video store air smelled like dust and stale popcorn. The fluorescent lights beamed down. I sweated under them, sure that the cashier would look at me next, would want a reaction.

I had wanted to touch the made-up man. Nothing weird, just the back of my thumb along his jaw, so his foundation barely skimmed off on my hand, just to let him know that somebody wanted to.

The cashier didn't flinch when I brought him my choices. Three horror movies: two originally Japanese—the really creepy shit that stays in your head because you can't figure it out easily—and one all-American with pop-out moments drenched in gore. Images to keep me up all night, so nothing else could.

Now, Lissie is snapping her fingers in front of my face. "Earth to Jackson, earth to Jackson," she's saying. She laughs, her mouth cat-tongue pink, her eyes green as jewels in the sun.

I jump to my feet, brushing loose grass from my lap.

"I'll be back."

I turn and start to walk toward the house. Even turned away, I can hear Lissie ask Taylor, "Does he usually just disappear like that?"

Even turned away, I can almost see Taylor's worn-out shrug. I slip inside, climb the stairs, drop on my bed, and pick up a book. A few minutes later, I hear their steps go softly by, toward Taylor's room at the end of the hall. I think one of the pairs of feet hesitates at my door for a breath, but I can't be sure.

At the mouth of the woods. We can see the house lights, bright spots in the foggy evening, but nobody knows where we are. Taylor's sneaked away some wine. She and Lissie have been out here for a while by the time I find them. "Welcome to the party!" Lissie declares, "Now all we need is Trevor. Where's the groom?" Lissie asks, finger-quoting the word.

"Out," Taylor says, blinking, her face flushed. "Come on, Jackson. It's my last night." She pours a glass for me and I take it with careful hands. Lissie clinks her glass against mine.

"So," she says, "We have wine. We have a tree," she gestures around. "We have blankets. Now what?"

"We could stargaze," Taylor says, giggling.

"Gay," Lissie denounces. "Trust me; I'd know. What do you wanna do, Jackson?"

I shrug. Lissie shakes her head. "What do you crazy kids do for fun when I'm not here?" She lies back between the two of us, both sitting cross-legged. Her hair spills across Taylor's lap. Taylor runs her fingers through, pulling out the tangles.

"We just sat around and missed you," Taylor says, "for years."

"Pathetic," Lissie says quietly, gazing through the gaps in the tree branches to the sky.

"A little." Taylor lets her hand fall along Lissie's ear and stay there.

"Jackson," Lissie says. A twig snaps as she rolls over, props herself up on her elbows so she's facing away from both of us, "Remember when I torture-kissed you?"

"What?" Taylor takes back her hand and turns to me.

"Jackson and I had a veritable affair," Lissie says. "A dalliance, if you will. Right before I moved to California. Remember when we tied him to the tree?"

"Mom grounded me for a week," Taylor says, laughing with relish. She plucks a sprig of pine needles from the ground and begins stripping them off their twig, one by one. "I didn't know you kissed him."

"Oh, I did."

"First kiss," I say, taking another sip of the wine. It seems like something you drink to.

"Why?" Taylor asks. The color is high in her cheeks. "Why him?"

Lissie laughs. "He was the prettiest boy I knew."

I blush, but they don't notice. Lissie clears her throat. So softly that I almost miss it, she says, "He looked just like you."

I glance back and forth between the two of them. They're both holding themselves very still, and neither of them will look at each other.

"Should I leave?"

"No," Taylor says, almost before I've ended the sentence. Lissie shrugs. A beat passes, and she rolls back over, sits back up. I can't see her expression in the shadow. "Let's play a game," she says.

Taylor swallows a gulp of wine. Lissie pulls the heavy bottle from its hollow in the dirt and refills Taylor's glass, then her own. Mine is barely touched. "You're gonna have to catch up with us, Jackson," she says. Before I can respond, she clears her throat.

"Let's play Truth or Dare."

"Truth," Taylor responds.

"Coward," Lissie says, "But very well. Taylor darling, bride-to-be—what is your biggest regret?"

Taylor sips meditatively, then smiles. "I don't want to answer that."

"Do you want a dare?"

"No." She sets her glass down, balancing its base between her sneakers.

She pulls back her hair with both hands, twisting it into a bun that falls out the second she lets go.

"Oh, I don't know. I guess I regret"—she glances at Lissie—"not traveling more. Trevor wants to buy a house as soon as we can afford it. I wanted to live in Paris."

"Have you told him that?" Lissie asks. Taylor shakes her head, her hair falling apart more against her shoulders.

"You should," Lissie says. The insides of her lips are stained.

"Truth or dare," Taylor says back, looking at the ground.

"It's Jackson's turn." Lissie reaches for the bottle again and tops off all of our glasses.

"Truth," I say.

"You two and your truths," Lissie says. Taylor looks at me, head tilted, eyes blank. "What should I ask?"

"What do you want to know?" Lissie shoves the bottle back in the dirt.

Taylor looks, hard, like she's trying to pierce through my head. Her lips are stained too. I rub my tongue over my teeth. She keeps staring and then hiccups and starts giggling. "Why are you so weird?" she asks and then gasps.

I shrug. "I guess I don't feel like I fit in."

"No," Lissie says, "More than that. Nobody fits in, not in high school."

"It's not that I don't fit in with anyone else." I gulp some wine. "I don't fit in with me, either."

Taylor looks up. "What do you mean?"

"Like," I say, "maybe I was supposed to be a—" I look down. I wonder if I can just stop talking. Lissie reaches awkwardly over Taylor to me and pats my shoulder. "Girl."

Taylor tilts her head and opens her mouth, but she doesn't say anything. She leans on Lissie's shoulder, clinking her glass meditatively against her teeth so the liquid rocks and sloshes.

"Now that," Lissie says "is how the game is played." Her voice is hard and bright, like glass. "Taylor, you could learn something from your brother."

Taylor rolls her eyes. "Fine, Lissie. Your turn."

"Dare."

I cough, clearing the shakes out of my voice. I cast my mind around the possibilities, but I can't think of a single dare.

"You can work together," she says, smirking. "Good luck finding anything I wouldn't do." She drains her glass and reaches toward the bottle.

"Kiss me," Taylor says, fast. She shuts her mouth, swallows and coughs.

Her face is flushed. She sucks her lips between her teeth, but she doesn't take it back.

Lissie looks at her with slitted eyes. "You're joking," she says. The words fall dull in the air. Taylor keeps staring.

"Fine."

Lissie unspools herself from her cross-legged ball on the ground. She crawls in the leaves, her foot catching against one of the branch walls, almost crashing the fort down into rubble. She sits on her knees, looking my sister dead in the eyes. She cradles Taylor's face in her dirty hands, tilts her chin up, and kisses her.

Taylor caves into the kiss and Lissie hunches over, sliding closer until they're gripping each other. I tip my glass up and tilt back until there's nothing left. After a moment, I stand up as quietly as I can and duck my big, awkward body under a low branch and into the open yard. I stretch out and take a full breath of cool night air. I look up at the tree-fringed sky, beaded with stars, and walk back, away from the edge of the woods and toward the light that spills from the kitchen window.

That night, I wake up feeling skittish and weird. I go downstairs for water, the stairs creaking as I descend them. A shadow in the empty kitchen falls oddly. When I flick on the light, it's Lissie, sitting in the window seat and smoking a cigarette. She has unhinged the top half of the window from its frame so she can sit huddled in the seat and the smoke escapes at the perfect angle.

"Hey, kid," she says, pursing her mouth to keep the cigarette in place while she waves.

"Hey, yourself," I say. "What brings a nice girl like you to a place like this?"

"Oh, I've seen my fair share of empty midnight kitchens, boy." She flicks ash into a coffee mug at her side and lets her breath out in a long sigh, a gust of fog against the window. I pull a tall glass from the cabinet and fill it with water. I watch Lissie watch the backyard. I switch to the ice dispenser, and it groans like a monster. Lissie looks at me, almost glaring. I can tell that she's trying to say something before she says it.

"Trevor's good to your sister, right?"

"Why wouldn't he be?"

"Not the right answer, kid."

"Stop calling me 'kid.'"

"Fair." She takes a long drag. "What I mean is—Taylor's making the right decision. Right?"

"She loves him," I say. Lissie nods. She drops the butt of her cigarette in a glass of water on the floor and rests her head against the glass. "Love, huh?"

She blows a lopsided smoke ring. "I might need you to remind me of that, okay? That she's making a good decision?"

"Sure," I say. "No problem." I look to her, but her forehead is pressed hard against the glass, and I figure if she wanted to talk, she could have knocked on my door instead of coming down and dismantling our window in the dark.

I fill my glass to the very brim and as I walk to the stairs, I try to keep it as stable as I can. Halfway up the stairs, I jolt and water pours over the side, soaking my shirt. I consider going down, getting a rag, refilling the water. I'm already halfway up, though, and Lissie doesn't seem like she's coming back upstairs for a while. The water will dry before anybody slips.

At the wedding rehearsal, Taylor is beautiful, Trevor is somber, and I'm exhausted. Lissie and I yawn through the ceremony and escape right after. We tell Mom that we'll be back in time for the dinner. "Okay," she says. "Aren't you two going to see if Taylor wants to come along?"

Lissie smiles with closed lips. "If you wouldn't mind, Mrs. Wright, could you just let her know we left when you see her?"

"Sure, sweetheart," Mom says—and then we're out the door. Lissie looks at me, and her face is back, her smile wide, her eyes suddenly exuberant. "I have an idea."

"What?"

"The tree," she says. "Where we tied you up."

I look at her, confused. She smiles harder. "Have you ever climbed it?"

"What are your dreams?" I ask, out of breath. Lissie's an ace climber—she's perched a few branches above me, snapping her gum and breaking twigs into smaller and smaller pieces. Specks of bark tumble into my hair and eyes, so I stopped looking up.

"Find a girlfriend. Get Internet famous. Travel to Saturn."

Fragments of bark sift down the back of my neck. "Internet famous?"

"You think I'm funny, right?"

"Sure."

"Thanks, I know. So, I'm planning on bringing the joy of my brilliant sense of humor to the world. Blogging, vlogging, et cetera."

"Oh."

"You may not know this, Miss Wood Nymph, but out in the world of social media, you can reach a thousand people without leaving your bedroom. It's pretty incredible."

"You want to reach people."

The leaves above me rustle as she shifts. "I don't want anyone to feel like they have to grow up alone. Like you," she says. A twig cracks. "Or like me."

She swings down, suddenly, to my branch, landing crouched. Wisps of her hair glow in the deepening sun. "Jackson," she says, "do you think you feel more trapped recently?"

I nod.

"Why do you think," she asks, "Taylor's getting married makes you feel trapped?"

"I don't know if it's that," I say.

"Weddings can be hard for some people." she says. "Misfits of a certain breed."

"You're the one who wanted to skip it, right?" I've kicked a rock, throwing me off her gait, a half-step behind.

"Right," she says. She looks at me for a long while before looking away. "It's getting dark," she says. "Let's go inside."

Lately, I'm so used to wedding frenzy. Without it, the house feels abandoned, holding depth and echo that I've been missing in the flurry. Lissie feels it too—when I reach to flip on the kitchen light, she says "Don't" in a sudden voice.

We pick our way through the downstairs giggling, bumping into furniture, hushing each other. When I find the stairs, I wait for her. I hold out my hand, and when she tucks hers inside it, I pull her up with me.

My room is densely shadowed, barely lit by the streetlight's steady glow. Occasional cars drive by, their headlights painting slow gold squares across the wall. Lissie shuts the door with a soft clink before she sits on my bed, then lies down, her thin body sleek against the mattress. Her face is hidden in pillows. I sit next to her, awkward. My weight and size feel as if they can veer out of control if I don't keep them tucked close.

"Hey," I say, trying to hold myself in.

"Hey." She slips her hand against my back and rubs soft circles between my shoulders. She feels fluid, like someone who can just glide and pool against other people without overthinking every move.

I lean back and turn away, and then turn back. I feel like a level, or a scale—too much, not enough, askew. She smirks, and her eyes flutter closed.

"It's okay," she says. She slips her hand in mine again and tugs me barely toward her. I tug back, and she pauses. "But also we don't have to," she says. But I'm sick of not doing, especially when I know that something, anything, has to change.

Lissie holds herself up over me, her palms against the bed. Her breath is mint gum and rehearsal dinner. Her cheek dimples and she oozes closer, sinks her small frame against mine. I am enjoying the press of her. I am sick with the press of me. I thought this might be something my body could be good for and apparently I thought wrong, but I am trying to stay in this moment and resist being deeply uncool and be here for her, make her happy or just not think so much. Is all.

I try to will my thoughts out of my body, but she leans in me, curve on bone. All I am is body right now and it feels good but wrong, and off, and unfair.

A gasp of tears surges in my throat. I can't speak through it. I skim my hands over the small of her back, wanting something else, and pretending that this is easy, and wishing as hard as I can that it wouldn't have to be pretending.

I try to stay here, to keep control. I try to feel her perfect skin and ignore that she's feeling the wrong thing back. Her hand urges my shirt over, off; my belt open, my zipper down. I strain toward her and away. I try to focus on kissing her neck, try to empty myself and just make her feel, but she presses harder and I want and the sick of my stomach is blank and I can't, I say, in a hoarse gasp as I push away.

Lissie's lips are wet. She licks them and bites, looking timid as her expression falls and then folds away. "I should have known better. I should have set boundaries." She turns over and draws into herself. "I push it too far," she mumbles into my pillow, "I always want too much."

I want to touch her, to pull her back—maybe not all the way into me, but back so I can see her face. But she's turned hard away, and the moment is already cracked open. I can't stuff it back shut. I'm too wrong for this.

I turn away too, and lie with my eyes open, waiting for something to change. Shadows ebb and sink along my wall. Cars drive by, casting filtered light through the window. Downstairs, my family comes back home, laughing but hushed—tired.

I wish we'd stayed. I wish we'd watched Taylor and Trevor be nauseating-cute. I wish I'd stuck around to watch my mom get sad-eyed and then smiley again. I wish I'd seen Taylor and Trevor dance together. I wish I'd stuck around to watch their befores. The more afters I see, the less I want to be involved with them.

I play a game with myself in which I gradually edge away from Lissie, wanting to see if she rolls or shifts to fill the space that I'm making between us. She stays still as a pond, breathing too evenly to be asleep. I wonder where the pigtailed girl who kissed me when we were nine went. I wonder if I've killed her.

Eventually, her weight lifts off the bed, creaks along the floor, turns the doorknob with quiet care, and slips away. I fall into timid, shaky sleep that pulls in and out of itself through the night, that can't tell its dreams from its memories.

When I wake up, the voices downstairs glow with laughter. I sit up, sigh into my rough-edged body, shuck off the dress slacks that I never changed out of. I shower. I close my eyes getting out. I look at my teeth in the mirror after I've brushed them; when I shave, I imagine that I can get cut so close to the root of my bristly skin that I can scrape to a smoother skin beneath. I pay attention to the eyes that stare out of me, that hold the past few days but don't reveal them.

As I creep down the stairs, Taylor gulps pancakes in unwieldy forkfuls, laughing wildly over something Lissie just said. I rub my eyes. Nothing changes. When Taylor bounces up to get more orange juice, Lissie half-smiles at me, shrugging. Mom sets me a plate between the two of them.

"Everything's okay?" I ask her, gesturing to Taylor.

"Guess so."

"Listen," I say, hushed, fast, "I want to talk about everything and fix it. I don't know how, but I want to."

Taylor plops back in her chair. "I'm just so happy!" She announces. A spot of syrup on her chin shines when she speaks. "Jackson," she says in an affected voice, "Did you know that I'm getting married today? Word is on the street," she agrees with herself, exaggerating her hands, "that I'm getting married today."

"I do declare," Lissie adds in a Southern-belle tone, "I just heard ever such a marvelous piece of news. I heard that Taylor Wright is getting married today. Did you ever hear such a pretty piece a gossip in your ever-lovin' life, Jackson?"

She winks at me, takes my hand under the table, and leans to the side as she smiles: wide, eager, and open. In the briefest glimpse, I swear I can see everything she didn't say and everything she wanted to.

"I do declare," I answer, smiling. I can feel my mouth stretch. "I never did hear any news so grand."

Nicholas Samaras

The Exiled Child Looks Back

Meaning every town I ever lived in.
Meaning every ghost village I walked out of.

Meaning the palpable air and weather
in the village I had to leave behind.

Meaning the history of the world I grew through.
The childhood bomb shelters. The summer

the city was burned for the colour of protest.
Meaning the military tanks on my front yard—

and this is literal. I touched the tanks
with my own hands, on my forced walk to the school bus.

Meaning the history of the world
I was required to move away from.

Meaning the school buildings that emptied
their glossy halls of my name, not even echoed.

Meaning moving for the sake of a parent's job or a life.
Meaning leaving everything I had been

and everything I was becoming. Meaning
growing into work that became being paid for doing a job you hated.

Meaning made meager by circumstance
until circumstance became meaning.

Meaning every world I moved from and moved from
and no girl ever cried for my leaving.

Angie Macri

Landlocked

No one is landlocked,
not even on the prairies
where water was drained,
earth lush as fire,

not on the high plains
where the aquifer walks
with the names of people gone:
Ogallala, Arikaree.

The mountain creeks
divide water between two seas.

Somber mother
with eyes the shade of wood,
somber father
who never knew where he stood,

your child became a chore,
wanting to know the name
of every bird,
especially on the old prairies,

where sparrows sang
of water long gone.

The Alligator Goes No Farther North than This[*]

For I've heard your voice
(wait, wait)
in the river's high water.
Steamboats from New Orleans
come in cotton, in silt.

For I've heard your voice
in the river that moves to other rivers,
the Red, the Black.
The swans arc
in winter.

I've heard your voice in boiling springs,
in cane and pine, ferruginous earth.

From the forks of the tiger,
the bayou of salt,
I've filled my voice with salt
in slate.
The band of red wolves was running.

From the tulip's hiding place,
the chute, the cache,
my voice became a cache
of spicewood, feverbush,
too hot for fingers to touch.

*The poem's title is taken from a notation on an 1804 map of the Ouachita River.

Robert Newman

Morning Coffee

I have a great deal of company in my house,
especially in the morning when nobody calls.
HENRY DAVID THOREAU, *Walden*

The clink of a spoon on the lip of a cup
the muddy surface rolls fertile like Nile silt
while dust drifts and robins gossip

The kitchen air a long-held breath
as a fly stutters against the window
desperate to get on with its last day

Michael Fessler

The Inner-Peace Initiative

A man, whom I had never seen before, slapped a small card down on the counter of the coffee shop in Bunkyo Ward, Tokyo. I frowned. When I'm *at window*, as I term it, I don't like being disturbed. That's why people do it, of course.

"Give me your reaction," the man said, "if you wouldn't mind."

On the card were the following three lines:

under the gingko
left at the persimmon
past the sundial

"Directions presumably," I said.
"You might say that."
"I did say that."
"You weren't certain though."

I looked at the man. I mean *looked*. He was slender. Blond hair. Oblong head with pointy features. In his forties, I guessed. No wrinkles. Wore a vest that could have used washing.

"Hard to please, aren't you?"

Was he a photojournalist or something? Did he have a camcorder and intend to make a film? *Expat at Window*. The docudrama. Sip. Sip. Sip.

"It's a haiku," he said.
"Right."
I read it again.
"Where does it lead?"
"Nowhere," he said.

"Been there many times," I chuckled and patted him on the shoulder in a burst of bonhomie. I could feel his bones. He was skimpy on the flesh.

"If I had specified the what or where, it would have killed the poem."

He moved his shoulders back and forth as if he were walking. But he was sitting.

"Okay, I take your point. It's open-ended."

"So you like it?"

"It has potential."

"C'mon, take a stand."

To think I had been placidly gazing out the window.

"I need a little time to adjust to the profundity of it," I said.

"No rush."

"Alone."

"You don't seem to be a loner. You have leadership qualities."

Oh, no.

"What's your name, if I may ask?"

"Stark," I said, against my better judgment. "Henry."

"Stark Henry, like Patrick Henry? Give me liberty?"

"Like Henry Stark. Give me a break."

He giggled.

"I'm Aurelius."

He flipped the card over. On the reverse was written:

Aurelius Fee. Buddhist Mind Reader & Haiku Poet

"I have no card," I said. "I don't believe in them."

"We have a little haiku group. Meet once a month. You're welcome to join us."

"Do you charge money?"

"Please?"

"Is there a fee?"

I meant that facetiously, of course. Given the name on the card.

"I often ask myself that," he said.

"You do?"

"I am Aurelius Fee, but is there really an Aurelius Fee?"

Cooperate. He could be dangerous.

"You might bulk out some," I suggested. "If you're really..."

"I mean, is there really an Aurelius Fee spiritually?" he glossed, which explained nothing.

"Yeah, well, there's really a Henry Stark."

"Demonstrably."

I suppose I had demonstrated it, but this was becoming unnecessarily abstruse. Or it was enough complexity for one sitting. Young Mr. Fee seemed to understand and he got up and left. Didn't even say goodbye.

Just walked out of Dream's Coffee. That was the slightly strange but evocative name of the café. It was a chain shop. I put his card in my book, which happened to be a collection of the writings of the Japanese haiku poet, Santoka. Had Santoka wondered if there was really a Santoka? Maybe he did.

I didn't connect with Fee for a long time after that. Well, not for six months. Six months is a long time when you're my age. That is, mid-sixties. You have to prioritize. You have to set reachable goals. It's probably too late to take up Sanskrit in any serious way, for example. But I keep busy. Do a lot of walking. Always have a book with me. That's my life. A book. A walk. A window. A coffee. Simple. One afternoon (it was now winter and bloody cold), I was in Bunkyo Ward again. There was a slight drizzle and I stopped at Dream's Coffee. I like the anonymity of the chains. I like the paper cups. I spotted a free seat by the window and claimed it (draped my coat over the stool and plopped down my book bag) and went to the counter for a self-service latte. The waitress patted my hand when she gave me the change. Felt great. I love pretty waitresses. I love getting change too. Someone was observing me.

"I knew you would come," Fee said.

"Did you?"

He tugged on his vest.

"Fee, that thing could use a washing."

"If I washed it, no one would recognize me."

"Point taken."

"Won't you join us?"

He indicated a table in the corner. Three tables really. Shoved together. A group of people were sitting around them. A haggard bunch, if I ever saw one. They looked about ready to expire.

"I generally drink my coffee alone . . . as you know."

One of the people at the table waved, beckoning.

"We need a fresh face."

"My face is not now nor has ever been fresh."

The whole table waved to me, as if they were calling for help.

"I'm not a joiner," I added.

We had drifted over to the table. I didn't recall moving.

"Henry Stark, everyone," Fee said.

I bowed slightly and a chair was pushed out. Whose leg did the pushing? Probably the tall wheezy guy's.

"Welcome to confusion," he said.

"Been there."

The wheezy guy was even older than I was. Aquiline nose. Dirty white mustache. Not exactly doddering but.

"You okay?" I asked.

"If you're okay, I'm okay," he said.

"I've never been okay."

"Win's on the way out," the man next to him informed me. "No win."

"George Winders," Aurelius supplied.

I nodded.

"And that's Clyde Norton," Fee said, indicating the other man.

Norton was sixtyish. Bristle brown hair. Ruddy complexion. Both he and Winders were Americans, judging from their accents.

"And this is Maya," Aurelius said, pointing to a Japanese woman.

She had haunting eyes. Had I seen her before? She wasn't bad looking. Fortyish. Thin. Personally I like a heftier woman. Anyway, George Winders, Clyde Norton, and Maya.

"Who are you?" I asked the silent Japanese man next to Maya.

"My..."

He had a large head. Bald on top. Tufts at the temple. I leaned forward, prompting him, but he didn't finish.

"That's Obuchi," Aurelius said.

Obuchi appeared to be on the dark side if not saturnine. If not Saturn himself.

"Used to sell insurance . . ." Winders said, and made a tiny space between his thumb and index finger to indicate the tentativeness of such a thing.

"Death insurance," he added.

I felt something moving under the table. I looked below and saw a thin man, Japanese, in a black top hat. He was fiddling with a sketch pad. Seemed to be searching for something. A pencil?

"Does he always—?"

"Not always. Not not always. That's Goro Goro."

I waved.

"Draws you out," Aurelius winked. "Deaf. Can't hear."

I took a seat next to Maya. She appeared to be the most stable of the bunch in spite of her stare, which was deep and gaping. You could fall into it.

"We were going over a haiku before you came in," Fee said. "Would you mind adjudicating?" He passed it over before I could refuse.

I bite into
a marshmallow
the sound of rain

"We need you to assess it without knowing whose it is," Clyde Norton said, coughing. He took out a handkerchief. "We want an objective point of view."

They wanted me to make an enemy, that is.

"It's the *kaki kueba* thing," I ventured. "Shiki bit into a persimmon and heard the temple bell at Horyuji, and the writer of this one has bitten into a marshmallow—"

"Cut the aesthetic crap."

"Win, if you don't mind. Henry's a guest today."

"Fee fie fiddly."

"Quite all right," I said. "Everyone's entitled to his opinion."

"Go ahead," Clyde Norton directed.

"Thank you. One might even say that the squish sounds like soft rain, or that the former caused the latter. Funny."

"You think haiku are funny?" Win objected.

"Droll perhaps."

"I quit," he said.

Why would he do that? His hand trembled and he hit the table to stop the shaking. Goro Goro, as if summoned (feeling the vibration?), came up from below and did a quick sketch of the group, including myself. Win struck a pose and then edged toward the door of the coffee shop. He may have been quitting, but he wanted to get into the sketch all the same. Had I offended him? Anyway, he left.

"It was his haiku."

"I didn't pan it."

"He always quits. It's his way of saying g'day, mate," Fee translated.

"Elvis has left the building," Norton said.

I chuckled.

"Clyde, what do you do for a living?"

He looked as if he were getting up there in years.

"I do for a dying."

Didn't we all?

"How about before that?"

"Commodities. Assigned to Japan. Now retired."

His accent sounded East Coast and I asked where exactly he was from.

"New York state. Lackawanna area."

"Never been there."

"No desire."

"Excuse me?"

"Lacka wanna."

"Got it."

"This is for you," Aurelius said, handing me the sketch that Goro Goro had made. "A souvenir. Don't feel obligated."

"To what?"

"Join our group."

"Not to worry."

I propped the sketch against my reference books. Goro Goro had flattered me. Shortened my nose. Added some symmetry that wasn't there. That was nice. The sketch was dated and signed, GG. Nonetheless, I wondered if I hadn't been co-opted. I should say that I've been a member of not a few haiku groups. To be candid, most of the ones I've joined (and subsequently resigned from—call them clubs, associations, *kukai*, cliques, coteries, what you will) have been composed of some pretty batty personalities. (I'm a little batty myself.) Haiku attracts eccentric types. Folks trying to stuff their feelings, if not their whole lives, into tercets of seventeen syllables. The group at Dream's Coffee Bunkyo Ward appeared to be in a category of its own, however. They were exceptionally contentious, if not hostile and even a little morbid. Winders, for one, was downright quarrelsome. Fee (the so-called "Buddhist mind reader") appeared to exercise some kind of authority over the others, but his role was ambiguous. All in all, it hardly seemed in my long-term interest to join the group. So naturally I did. In a way, I did. But more on that anon.

"I knew you would be here."

At Dream's Coffee, he meant.

"Did you?"

The hands at the table went up, beckoning.

"Henry *sensei*," Fee said to everyone.

"Just Henry," I corrected.

Maya stared at me. She was like one of those portraits whose eyes follow you when you're trying to leave a museum. Obuchi didn't seem to be around today. Goro Goro was under the table. (I looked.)

"What did you mean by this?" Clyde Norton demanded.

"Mean by what?" I asked.

He placed one of my haiku down on the table. It was from *Haiku Futures*. Best-of issue. Fee's group had been checking up on me.

to be in
a preponderance of green
the wind active

"Oh," I said, dismissing it. "Not much of a haiku."

"Why state the obvious?" George Winders said, shaking.

"But it did win Best—"

"Best is bullshit."

I didn't swear by prizes either, but I had never turned one down.

"What's it mean?" Norton prodded. He seemed to have lost some weight. He was aggressive though. No lacka wanna.

"It just means that I felt like taking a walk into the green woods to feel the breeze. I phrased it in an unusual way. Gave it a twist."

"Why didn't you just say what you meant?"

"Yeah," Win said, and made a monkey face, exposing his gums.

I turned to Fee. He fingered his vest. I wasn't even a member of the group. I pointed that out.

"Don't kid yourself," Win said. "You're one of us."

That gave me pause.

"I originally had *Oh* at the beginning," I conceded. "*Oh, to be*, et cetera..."

"Why did you cut it?" Clyde demanded.

"He lacked the courage of his convictions," Win answered for me.

"*Au contraire*," I said, defending my haiku. "*Oh* seemed excessively wistful. *Oh to be*... How many poems begin that way?"

"You tell us," Win said.

"A fair number."

Goro Goro popped up and held his pencil out in front of him, centering the scene the way artists do. He bumped his top hat on the way down.

"So you think minimal is better?" Clyde asked. "Is that what you're saying?"

"Minimal criminal," Win rapped.

"Not so much minimal as *gendai*," I said. "Contemporary, that is."

I looked around the coffee shop. Were people listening in?

"It's just a haiku," I added.

"Just?"

"Poetic diversion. That's one way of looking at it."

"We're not effete types," Clyde said. "We're concerned with what's real."

"Poetic diversion is bullshit," Win interjected, showing his teeth again.

"Wait a minute," I said, taking cover. "I resent that."

Aurelius sat there complacently. He might have intervened on my behalf.

"You see, we've read your stuff," Clyde explained. "We study the journals."

"I'm flattered."

I wasn't actually. I was wary.

"Writing is dead serious," Win stated.

"Look, guys, for some writers haiku is a kind of therapy, but I don't look at it that way. I don't dismiss the idea, but it's not my view."

"What's your view?"

"Haiku is art."

"It's life and death," Win countered, his voice splitting.

I made some feeble rejoinder and scanned the table and met Maya's eyes.

"WA!" she said.

That's the Japanese equivalent of BOO!

The next week I phoned Fee. His *keitai*, or cell phone, number was printed on the card he'd given me at Dream's Coffee. In small print. I'd overlooked it. I fished the card out of the edition of Santoka's haiku.

"Oh, yes, I was expecting your call," he said.

"Were you?"

I added, "I'm the guy your fellow members attacked."

"Just their way of being friendly."

"Oh, is that what it was?"

"Pugnacity is a kind of compliment."

"In dystopia."

He told me that I had conducted myself well under the circumstances.

"Well, you can't say Maya didn't say WA."

That gave him something to disentangle and he went silent. Probably thought he was reading my mind.

"Incidentally, Fee, are you walking around?"

There was no such thing as a stationary call anymore. People needed to pace about (and be seen pacing about) with their mobiles stuck to their heads.

"*Sensei*, the next time—"

"I'm not your *sensei*, Fee. And no next time. That's why I'm calling."

"But you're reading Santoka."

"Am I?"
"You are."
I wasn't.
"In a way, you are," he said.
"In a way, angles are arcs. What's your point?"
"Santoka put art aside and lived haiku."
"He wrote simply, but nothing simple is simple."
"What about:

unconditioned air ah

"Fee, I'd appreciate it if you wouldn't cite my *ku* to me over the phone."
"Santoka would have understood that haiku."
"Would he?"
"Yes, it's about someone gasping for weather. Weather is real."
"Fee, you know what?"
"No, I don't know what. I'm trying to determine if I am really I. Remember?"
"Only too well. Someday I'm going to recite your work back to you."
"Far inferior to anything of yours."
"No one's work is inferior to mine."
"The group needs you."
"They need—"
But he put me on hold. I twirled my pencil. I was at home, stationary, and surrounded by what is now referred to as *print*. Real books, that is.
"Sounds like naive realism," Fee said, returning.
Maybe he *could* read minds.
"Obuchi won't be coming."
"Is that any concern of mine?"
"C'mon, Henry."
"Obuchi uttered only one word last time."
"He won't ever be coming."
"Hardly a loss, is it?"
There was a pause.
"Could you join us, as a favor. I need a little support."

I have another life. I teach at the U. I won't go into that except to say it pays my way and keeps me mentally nimble (or mentally on edge). My classes are regarded as breaks from learning. Haiku writing has filled the gap in my existence. Initially I did not take the genre seriously (some people say I still don't) but gradually that changed. Small is beautiful. Less is more. Unconditioned air ah. I have a few chapbooks to my name. I don't advertise my successes. The fact that Fee's group had actually located and scrutinized individual haiku of mine and were focusing on them was baffling. Moreover, their choices were highly idiosyncratic. They seemed to be fixed on my experimental *gendai* stuff, though I wrote traditional haiku as well. In any event, I decided to hang in there. Not to disengage. Fee was a person in need of support if there ever was one. The man didn't even know if he was Fee. If things got too crazy, I could bug out. I hadn't signed a contract.

"So you couldn't stay away, could you?"

Win heaved the words, pushing hard to get them out. Shortness of breath, I guessed. It was mid-afternoon. Downtime at Dream's Coffee.

"You need us," he said.

"Do I?"

"Don't be so cavalier."

"Cavaliers ride, Win. I'm a walker. Walk everywhere, all over Tokyo."

"Okay, you're showy."

Obuchi wasn't around, as Aurelius had said he wouldn't be. Goro Goro was under the table. (I checked.)

"Maya," I nodded. Her cheekbones were more prominent than before. It had been only a month since I'd last seen her. Not even that long.

"Clyde," I said to Norton.

He raised his coffee cup. Wobbled it slightly. Hurried it. Slopped it.

"What's today's topic?" I queried.

Aurelius said that the members wanted to tap my expertise. He tugged on his vest. The clammy thing.

"Really, Fee—"

"It's my *samsara* vest."

"You have an appointment in *samsara*."

"He doesn't hide the dirt," Win countered.

"I'm clean," I said.

Not exactly a retort.

Clyde pulled out a copy of the current *haiku futures*, pleated it, and read:

after asparagus bear urine

I covered my eyes.

"Meant to be facetious," I said. "For the record, that would be the chemical methyl mercaptan."

"What do you know about chemicals?"

"Not much, Win. That's why I called it—"

I held my nose.

"You give enough urine samples and . . ."

Win trailed off. Maya took his hand. Her eyes popped a little.

"Would anybody else have a haiku to show around?" I asked. "No need to focus on my stuff exclusively. Or ever."

Win stood, trembled, excused himself, and shuffled off to the Gents.

"To be honest, George doesn't write many haiku anymore," Norton said.

"Why not?"

"Takes too much energy."

"Really? Three lines. *I bite into a marshmallow* wasn't bad."

Maya gaped. Clyde coughed. I coughed. Seemed like the polite thing to do.

"*Gents*, my butt," Win huffed, returning to the table.

Aurelius held the chair for him. Clyde started coughing again. I didn't accompany him this time.

"You still working?"

"Teach at the university, Win."

He reached for a paper napkin, mopped his mouth with it, wadded it up.

"Ever drool?"

He exposed his yellow teeth.

"So far, so good," I said.

Wouldn't my students have a chuckle. If I drooled. On their essays.

"You teach them haiku?"

"Rarely. They think haiku are NGNP. No Gaijin Need Apply."

"We've got some other haiku of yours that we'd like to get to," Clyde said.

I covered my head with the menu.

"Leave it," Win said. "Enough bear urine."

"George, you need some help?"

Win was now standing but unsteadily. He had some haiku journals in his arms and was struggling to keep them from slipping onto the floor.

"I quit," he said.

I offered to accompany him to the station.

"Accompany yourself."

He hobbled out of Dream's Coffee. At least he wasn't anodyne. Of course, he was ill. They all were. I had finally put it together.

MICHAEL FESSLER

Clyde, Maya, and Goro Goro (who tipped his top hat) filed out. It had been an abbreviated session. Aurelius stayed behind. He shrugged and exhaled.

"Fee, I think it's time for you to fill me in on the details. From the beginning..."

Why I hadn't pressed him before this, I can't say. Maybe I'd been in Nippon too long. Unpleasantness is always kept out of sight here. Anyway, this is what Aurelius told me. He had first come to Japan a decade ago as a financial consultant for Poynders-Shimura. His Nihongo was good—he had studied the language at UC Berkeley—and he had connections: his mother was a Poynders. He worked at the firm for several years but became dissatisfied with the financial market milieu—credit ratings, Nikkei averages. "Indicators that indicated nothing," he said. He took a leave of absence. The hiatus lasted longer than expected and resulted in his quitting Poynders-Shimura to join an NGO with a branch in Japan. That lasted a year. Subsequently he floated around Asia and "got funky." He was searching for something. He called his search "the inner-peace initiative."

"There was turmoil up here," he told me, and tapped his head.

While walking in Bunkyo Ward one day (he had returned to Japan), Aurelius wandered into a temple where he struck up an acquaintance with the abbot. (Not your conventional head priest—the man doubled as a DJ on weekends.) They had a number of serious, and unserious, talks and the abbot invited Aurelius to stay at the hut on the grounds. He accepted. Wakoji, he soon found out, was a "healing temple." That is, people came there to pray for well-being and recovery. After he had been in residence for some months, a delegation contacted the abbot and asked if Aurelius might not be deputed to speak with them from time to time in English. They were all terminal cases.

"They figured Japanese wouldn't be spoken in the next life," Aurelius chuckled.

"What was the haiku connection?" I asked.

"Adventitious," he said.

The sessions were conducted in the hut on the grounds. There was a rapid turnover naturally, but early on one of the members who happened to be a haiku poet (now passed on) suggested that reading and writing haiku in English might be salutary for the members.

"Did you know anything about haiku at the time?"

"Not a thing."

"So you were just the person for the job."

"I was preparing them for heaven."

Many of the poems (*jisei no ku,* or death-haiku) that the patients contributed were unbearably beautiful: the shape of a stone, the tilt of a stem, all tinged with sadness but displaying remarkable restraint. Whenever possible, Aurelius took the groups on haiku-walks. ("Haiku-hobbles.") They stopped at coffee shops. That was something he inaugurated.

"How did non-Japanese come to be included?"

"The word went forth."

"And the abbot okayed it?"

"He said I needed to work out my salvation."

"How many groups have you gone through?"

"Depends on how you count them. Ten . . . about."

"You're still living at the hut?"

"Yes, it's just up the road."

He jerked his thumb and said, "Under the gingko, left at the persimmon, past the sundial."

"Directions to nowhere. And you want me to take over for you, is that it?"

Fee studied his hands.

"I don't know what I want."

Clyde Norton's shirt was too big for him. It didn't exactly hang on his body and you might not have noticed if you didn't know, but he had grown thinner and the shirt was no longer the right size. The gruffness of his manner hadn't abated though. "This haiku of yours," he said, and read from *Haiku Now*:

the quadrangle
is not bosky
I am gray concrete

"Your epitaph?"

"No, I was just having an off day at the U."

"So what was the problem?"

"I felt like a sidewalk. People walking all over me. Perhaps it was an epitaph for that particular day—you could say that."

"You don't know what an off day is!" George Winders jabbed.

He resembled a great white egret. Long thin neck. A single tuft of white hair stuck out from the crown of his head.

"What's an off day?" he prodded. "Tell us."

"Students chattering. Texting on their cell phones."

MICHAEL FESSLER   125

"That's an *on* day."

"Not when you're trying to deliver a lecture, Win."

"You need too much attention."

"I need some attention. The positive kind."

He drooled a little. Wiped it off with the back of his hand. Left a trail.

"Were you a smoker, Win?"

"I always gave them license, when I taught," he said, ignoring my question.

"All kinds of teachers, Win. I didn't know you were one too."

The tip of Goro Goro's hat pushed up from below and sank back.

"I was a handsome devil," Win said, drifting.

Norton shook his head.

"You look okay, George," he said.

No one else called Win that. They talked for a while about the latter's appearance. What the two of them had in common—perhaps the only thing—was that they were both ending their days in a foreign country.

I took a break and went to the counter with my cup, opened a packet of sugar, held it upside down over my coffee, stirred it in, and then dropped the packet—sayonara, baby—into the disposal. I went over my receipt. There was all kinds of information on it. Time. Day. Address. Transaction. I slipped it into my shirt pocket. Proof of some kind. In case I had to verify where I'd been today. I suppose I was avoiding going back to the table.

"You finished?" Win asked when I sat down.

"More or less."

I tapped my cup.

"Refined sugar, thrilling but killing."

"You have a lifetime to waste."

I was glad to hear it.

"Say, where's Maya?"

I looked around, noticing her absence for the first time. Win became reflective.

"She was a fine woman," he said.

He was having trouble swallowing. Choked. We waited for him to clear his throat. Took a while.

"You and Maya have something going?"

"None of your damn business, fruit."

"Just asking, Win. I'm not a fruit."

Aurelius patted him on the back. "Bad day, Win?"

"When I wanted a woman, nothing could stop me . . ."

Win was somewhere else. He sucked on his yellow buck teeth. Dropped his head into his hands.

"I cared! I was deep," he said.

He lifted his head as if dredging it up from a lagoon.

"I was deep," he repeated. "Not like you," he said, pointing at me.

"George is right," Norton reasoned.

"He is?"

"You've written your death poem and don't even know it."

"Just a gray day at the university, Clyde. I told you that. Most are."

Norton paused. He sat absolutely still for a moment, as if he were fighting off acute pain. Something in the chest area. Maybe the conversation had brought it on. He'd worked himself up.

"Sorry, Clyde, I don't do tragedy," I said to him after the incident had passed, or seemed to have.

"You don't do tragedy," Win almost shouted. "Tragedy does you!"

Things were flying. I figured I cared as much as anybody about his fellows, but now wasn't the time to argue the point. I turned to Aurelius who had sagged down in his seat. No help there. I'd probably have to carry *him* out. Our table had now gone dead silent. All around us the business of the café, as if someone had turned up the volume, was becoming clearer and more distinct. Spoons banging. Cutlery cutting. Forks striking plates. The fury of an espresso machine. The shrill timbre of table talk. And then suddenly Win rasping, catching his breath. I took the receipt out of my pocket and turned it over. It said: *Have a nice day and thank you for smiles.*

The university was on break and I was in Bunkyo Ward to meet with Fee. After exiting from the train station nearest Wakoji, I removed his card from my pocket and read it again:

under the gingko
left at the persimmon
past the sundial

I found the gingko easily enough. Now that it was winter it was leafless, as was the persimmon. The *hidokei*, or sun-clock, located in a clearing farther along, was mounted on a stone slab. Animals of the Chinese zodiac representing the times of day had been carved on the face. It had no motto. I thought of the famous inscription I had studied at school decades ago: *omnes vulnerant ultima necat.* All wound; the last kills. A reference to the hours. Given recent events, I wasn't surprised that I had recalled it. I slipped past the sundial, walked beneath the main gate, and entered the grounds of Wako Temple. The figure of Yakushi Nyorai was housed in the central building: one hand was raised in the Fear Not mudra; the other hand was holding a bowl. I bowed. At the back of the grounds was a small pond. The ice on it had cracked so that the surface looked like a broken window. Not far away was the hut.

"*Agatte kudasai*," Aurelius called from within when I knocked. Step up, that is. The door slid open. I stooped, entered, and stepped down. A small oil heater stood in the center of the room. In the corner was a *kiri no tansu* (paulownia chest). A few books had been stacked on top of it. What looked like Buddhist writings. Sutras, I presumed. Aurelius was wearing a *hanten*, or padded coat, over his "samsara vest." He poured me a cup of tea.

"Where's the boss?"

"Fund raising. Upping the cost of burial plots again."

"You doing okay?"

"Not sensational."

Clyde Norton had passed away in his sleep the previous week.

"How did Win take it?"

"Hurting."

Aurelius shifted and leaned against one of the poles. What must it have been like when a whole group was present in such a constricted space—and each person reciting a death poem?

"If one's mind is empty . . ."

"Emptiness clutters the mind," I said a little impatiently.

Fee tapped the paulownia chest. *Kiri* was reputed to burn more slowly than other woods and was therefore used for storing important articles. Maybe there was an allegory there.

"You need a change of venue, Aurelius."

I slapped him on the knee. Perhaps my jocularity was unfeeling.

He shrugged. There wasn't a wrinkle on his face. Not a worry line anywhere. What did that indicate? Was it the face he deserved? The Orwell thing? He certainly wasn't unreflective. You sometimes forgot that he was a wealthy man (the Poynders money) and didn't need to practice austerity. But he had lost some of his spunk and pluck, and needed to get out.

"I can't go until I find a replacement," he said, coughing theatrically. "Someone sufficiently spiritual."

"Disqualifies me."

"It's an opportunity, Henry."

I shook my head.

"No, I was born to pencil comments into the margins of student essays—and then complain about it."

Fee and I went back and forth on the topics of spirituality, emptiness, et cetera, for a good two hours, but neither of us budged nor changed his point of view. As I was walking to the train station later, I stopped and wrote:

clouds
coulds

A minimal haiku. Maybe not even that. But it summed up my feelings.

It was a frigid day in late January. Win and Aurelius came into Dream's Coffee in Bunkyo Ward and took a seat. Win wasn't looking good. He was pissed off, of course. His anger was his personality. It was what held him together.

"You make me sick," he said.

I smiled. Not a big smile.

"I'll put that on my tombstone," I said.

"You think you're witty, don't you?"

"With all the drawbacks that entails, Win. Wearing one's heart on one's sleeve wears out the sleeve."

"Stuff it."

Not my best, no.

Aurelius got up and went to the counter. As he was standing in line, he consulted his cell and called to us that Goro Goro was indisposed and wouldn't be coming today.

"Sorry to hear about Clyde," I said to Win.

The coffee shop seemed empty without his gruffness.

"He was a leader," I said, and added as a flourish, "of men."

"And you're a liter of piss."

I recoiled slightly.

"You need some pain in your life and you'll get it."

He was supplying it.

"What makes you think you suffer more than others, Win? Just curious."

"Eh?"

"It's illusion to think—"

I dropped the subject. Unfeeling of me under the circumstances. I wondered if I weren't a stand-in for someone from Win's past. An irksome relative or some such thing? But perhaps it was altogether simpler: I wasn't dying just now, and he was. It was a cruel thought but I couldn't dispel it.

"Illusion is bullshit," he said.

Pretty much summed it up. Aurelius returned with two espressos and put one in front of Win. A formality. He couldn't drink it. It was his permit to stay.

"Would you like me to leave?" I asked, "If I'm making you uncomfortable . . ."

"No, I'll leave."

He paused.

"When I go, I'll leave a deposit in your commode."

He coughed. Tossed up some stuff. Off-putting as imaginable. So much for comforting the afflicted. Aurelius asked if he were in pain.

"I'm in pain when I see his face," he wheezed.

I looked down. What was protocol anyway?

"I'm in pain because I'm leaving and he's staying, when if life had any meaning and was fair, it would be the reverse. I'm in pain when . . ."

He held his throat.

". . . I'm in pain all the time."

"Yeah, yeah, yeah," I said, surfeited. Immediately after saying it, I felt ashamed. I had lost control. Win lifted his head, stunned that I had answered back. Aurelius rubbed him on the shoulder softly.

"You're nothing," he sneered.

"I affect different people in different ways," I said.

I lapsed into silence. In spite of the animadversions, I had no ill feelings for Win. He was who he was.

"I don't want to go where people don't argue," he said.

Point taken. No one on edge and people endlessly patting one another on the back—wouldn't be much fun.

"Sweet Anodyne," he sang eerily. "My Anodynnnne . . ."

K132 was empty. No students around. It was so quiet you could hear a paperclip drop. (I dropped one, heard it. QED.) The room was the shabbiest on campus, but each year I requested it. They called it Stark's Room. I liked to think that the exchange of ideas that took place in it made it exciting and even luxurious. Passionate discussion was the best decor. Another illusion, of course. I shrugged. George Winders had died a month ago now. He had not gone "gentle into that good night." I picked up a piece of chalk and wrote on the board:

consciousness and then

I couldn't continue. Frustrating. People in my position were supposed to be plausible and even profound on such topics. But what came after *consciousness*? What was the answer to: *and then*? An eternity of altercation, as Win had referred to? Peace, justice, and harps? The young Liz Taylor on a silver serving dish? Clod-hood? White noise? I went to erase the words but instead left them up. Maybe someone (maintenance? a student?) would come along and complete the thought, thus unlocking the secret, tra-la, of human existence. Until then, I figured I knew as much about the topic as anyone. That is, nothing.

Sands from Mongolia and northern China, borne along on the spring winds, were sweeping through the Tokyo area. The phenomenon was known in Japanese as *Kosa*. Industrial pollution was part of the mix. Being out in it was a little like being out in a toxic milkshake. But Fee had emailed me and I had come to meet with him. I walked under the gingko, went left at the persimmon, passed the sundial, entered the grounds of Wako Temple and made my way to the hut. *Agatte kudasai*, Fee called out, and I entered. The kerosene heater was glowing. There was a kettle on top of it, water boiling. I took a seat on a cushion.

"I've followed your advice, Henry."

"What advice, Aurelius?"

"I've asked the abbot to release me from my obligations. I'm going back to America! I wanted to tell you."

"How did the abbot take it?"

"With profound equanimity."

"You're certain of that?"

"I'm a mind reader, remember?"

"I'd forgotten."

He removed a block of pu-ehr tea from the shelf, shaved off some leaves, placed them in an old pot, and poured in boiling water from the kettle. We waited as the tea steeped. Waited in silence, though neither of us was known for it. Finally, he produced two cups from beneath a patterned cloth, filled them, and passed one over.

"Fee, what have you learned from all this, now that you're leaving it?"

I swung my arm around in a wide arc.

"Oh, you know, how to die," he chuckled. "That sort of thing."

I chuckled back.

"Nothing like dying. How?"

He hemmed and hawed.

"I can't explain."

"Because it's inexplicable."

"Death is a once in a lifetime experience," he remarked cleverly.

"Well, you did good, Aurelius. You helped people. You eased their way."

Actually, I didn't believe that his searching, the so-called "inner-peace initiative," was quite over yet but kept that to myself. His pluck and spunk seemed to be returning. That was the important thing. Perhaps the thought of the Poynders money had something to do with it. In any event, we sat there chatting and drinking our Chinese tea for a good part of the afternoon, getting nowhere in particular but enjoying the exchange of ideas. Now and then bamboo grass brushed against the roof, creating a kind of wind music. Aurelius thanked me for helping him and reminded me that the position of leader was still vacant. I declined as before. When it was time to leave, I rose and made a few avuncular remarks. Then we bowed to one another.

"By the way," he said, and pulled open one of the drawers of the paulownia chest. "It was just this past week . . . He wanted you to have this."

Aurelius passed the top hat over.

So Goro Goro had been the last to go.

Todd Fredson

Heckling Paradise

Adam, you remember the zoo
unmaintained since the fighting,
as Abidjan became selectively abandoned?

Remember, in our villages, those cinder-block
houses unroofed since the economy stalled—weeds grown up
inside higher than the walls?

I close my eyes and rearrange what's left here.
That Frenchman who belched at the alligators,
dragged his Ivorian prostitute away by the hip.

The two lions that rolled their eyes on the broken
concrete slab as I stuck my hand through the bars.

The monkeys won't even play with themselves. You said
won't tug their red dicks?

I wanted to rip out my heart
and throw it to them.

We joked when the turtle poked its beak through the pond scum,
bathtub fart–bubble head.

Would it be too sentimental
to add the civette
prowling with one lost leg? Yet true.
You said this all simply:

Life is dangerous
under these blue skies.

And I learned with my slight smile—
scuttle, attrition . . . whatever is wild has been wild
by a matter of permissions;
willingness to hurt and to be hurt.

Consider the turtle, *in situ*.
Hours ferrying itself through loaves of foam,
it digs a nesting trench. Back and forth to the surf,
staying lubricated as it lays its eggs.

But that's the idea—with the zoo, you're stuck there.

Anniversaire

Rain
on the full moon's
high tide, rain
on the bulb of driftwood.

The first time
you want to hear a voice
any voice will do.

The birds
peck you apart, pole star
weighted
somewhere in their guts.

History Offers No Instruction

Slow enough to keep from sweating
but fast enough to keep the flies off my neck
I learned to walk in those years, which were endless years.
Mothers yelled, and I woke in the thick heat.
"Ka dah!" They clapped their buckets down the path.
The children peering over my window ledge

dropped in chase. I wiped sleep from the ledge
of my face, rolled onto the concrete sweating
already. A nannie bleats on this side of the path.
Goats' call and response next—
Hear the kid's panicked nattering? This heat
will have emptied my water basin, mineral rings like years

of scree marks on an expanding shore, years
ticked like rice across the bottom of a pot. Let
yourself watch—*Ee dah ka fei blei nah. Eat
here with me!* Benét will stop. Slosh sweating
down her bucket, tracing streaks on her neck.
From her ears, drops pock dusty leaves. The path

is clogged, Consti and Simone wade a new path
around Benét. Her gaze follows me. Fourteen years—
like some purple-winged bird twisting its neck
for my arrival. But I never—until with this ledger
In courtyards the cacao is spread for "sweating."
We only pay for these beans that have dried in the heat.

Once, maybe, I was really there. Above Benét's heart,
a *pagne* knot. And her baby behind bounces over the path.
"The gendarmes picked on a particular woman and
grabbed her breasts and started pulling her in circles . . .

Then told five boys to get an erection and rape the women . . .
took their penis in the palm of their hands and hit it,

hard, with the buckle of his belt." Am I, I am, nicked.
And you, you've not heard how stout the heat?
The new president fumbles the *bouchon de liege*
promising to outpace the past. A well-heeled path:
if intervention, and if traders, if the market bears
the new labor. As technologies sweeten.

The nurse's wet tin roof. The pump's handle and neck.
The glare paints your eyes shut. Years stammer, the heat
breaks—rain stomps that distance back into a single edge.

A Toast

Between each of the streams
there is a flower.
In the sand and gravel

between each
of the nine streams
a flower

for each of the boys,
a flower for each of the
nine I have become.

Kira Taylor

Turkey Vultures

Vultures are born without a voice,
the fold that is the thrush's flute;
they speak instead the language of the dead,
a lax whistle through the open pipes
of their throats as they circle low,
and lower still.

Their name means *tearer*, and also *purifier*—
through this rending, sun can dry the bones,
leave them stacked on the shore.

There are at least ten,
maybe a hundred in the ash trees;
from the low bend in the Skagit,
they look like fishermen.

Our boat: Charon's vessel, or the Khufu ship,
curved cedar bow buried with a pharaoh,

or Naglfar, built from the dead's
fingernails, and we
are parting tides to battle gods,
their black wings bright as they all
suddenly rise.

Joseph Bathanti

Emerson Street

This is the exact spot
on Emerson Street,
where August Dolan kicked me

so spectacularly in the balls.
I dropped to my knees, whispered *Oh*
and coughed out a baby blackbird—

the aftermath of my innocence,
that flew off and took its place
in the sycamores with the other crows

gathered to witness my revenge.
Dolan twisted out of his coat,
but I grabbed his tie,

garroting him one-handed,
sizing up his reddening face with my free fist.
Even now I feel with pleasure his fat

cheek blacken on my knuckles.
Sister Aloysius Gonzaga,
Sacred Heart's simian principal—

she favored Zira,
the hazel-eyed chimpanzee
animal psychologist played by Kim

Hunter in *Planet of the Apes*—
witnessed the entire affair
from her office, hauled us in,

backhanded Augie so hard
his scorched face peeled by lunch,
knocked us both into the marble stairwell

with a titanium yardstick,
then whaled the Communion
of Saints out of us as we lay there—

prompting the life-size statue
of Our Lady of Perpetual Help
to jitter on her plinth,

though she winked
when I gazed up at her in my stupor.
Birds have testicles,

but keep them hidden,
out of harm's way,
inside their bodies.

The North Game

Dulce et decorum est pro patria mori
HORACE, by way of Wilfred Owen's "Dulce et Decorum Est"

Off the Quadrangle,
the statue of Our Lady of Victory
presides like a warhead on its launch pad.
Through a portal secreted in ivy,

we enter the Christian Brothers hermitage,
then wind the vault down
into its medieval chapel:
coal-dim-glisten, ruby ether,

smoking iconography,
the reek of myrrh and niter.
The altar: lacy lambrequin;
solid gold cross, like a Roman short sword;

chalice, pall and purificator,
chalice veil; ciborium, paten;
cruets of amber Tokay.
At Coach Wheeler's command,

we forty-four kneel.
Father Pilarski, a Navy priest,
says Mass, in white vestments,
the symbol of innocence and triumph—

though it seems a ruse
this season of Requiem:
Calley on trial for Mylai.
Father prays God we win,

in expiation of our sins,
that we come away whole
in person and faith. United
in that desire, we step to the rail,

take upon our tongues the Eucharist;
then file, silent, through the minuscule
narthex where the bronze tablet
lists its roll of faithfully departed,

in relief, above the cast iron holy water font:
dead boys from the old wars—

World Wars I and II, Korea, and now
the inaugural names of our war, Vietnam.

We chant vespers, dirge out the Alma Mater—
Under your Towers moves life's eternal May—
as we march down the ramp to the bus,
toting sea bags:

helmets, spikes, pads,
blue and gold game jerseys—
the commingled remains
of all that's been forgotten.

We have no idea what we will walk into,
once we cross that colossal bridge
over the Allegheny—
where plenty of kids lose heart;

others, their minds; even
their eternal souls—to play the Trojans,
those animals from the North Side.
We have no choice.

We've taken an oath.
Those of us who return:
our parents and girls will be waiting
in the school cafeteria.

They'll rise and applaud as we stagger in.
On its run along the river,
a freighter howls.
Endless mills mass black and smoldering,

forging ample steel
to convene the Apocalypse.
The clocks have been turned back:
five o'clock. It's pitch black.

Haircut

Bagnio Vicas's barbershop
wedged the triune nexus of Omega Street,

Hoeveler Bridge, and Hamilton Avenue,
its ceremonial striped helix

of whirling red, white, and blue,
like prelude to a dream:

Bagnio in broken English
admonishing me to "Sit still" on the booster

lanced across the porcelain arms
of the chrome chair, jacked

with his lever, swiveled on a whim,
revved silver clippers boiling

at my nape, dun strop, heavy-
hanging, cadaverous, upon which he scourged

his pearl-handled straight razor.
He'd slice my throat if I didn't mind—

the way he spun my head in his gorgeous
hands, manicured cuticles, nails

precisely filed, fey as the Pope's
Pontifical purple gloves; blinding

white-belted *tunica*; the disintegration
of a Lucky Strike, an inch from my eye,

in his smoking lips,
the white scar bisecting them—

reminder of the One True Cross.
Bagnio, Calabrian Cary Grant,

nightshade lethal—
though fairy, some whispered.

He seemed nothing like a fairy—
more Captain Hook, with his choir of asses.

My mother loathed him, *gavone*,
gangster-pretty, boot-black razor-cut.

She had his number—
his beautiful wife was a tramp—

even if he did sing angelically *La Boheme*
as he pecked at my ears, slant smile

that necromanced Divine Providence
postulants strolling past his shop to the convent.

The hot lather cruet burbled Godlessly.
He owned the torch and candles, salves

and unguents. Negroes came to him
for fire cuts, processes—in confidence,

secret as a laboratory.
Tonsorial stench.

Labyrinthine mirrors.
Hair sprouted from his floor.

In the back room, with the brooms:
pornography.

I coveted the pink casket of Bazooka
he rewarded me with, the sugar-

powdered shrunken comic pressed in with it:
Bazooka Joe and his Magic Circle Club.

I sent away for the decoder ring.
I swore an oath. My father,

on the elevated shine stand, kept vigil.
He knew I hated Bagnio's black scissors,

its blind rat-tail eye, flying at me
like Hitchcock's grackles.

He held my hand
as we crossed Hamilton

to the listing Spignos Club
for rigatoni, and Tom Tucker pop—

the legend, *Spignos Saturnia*,
chiseled in the Tuscan tile

crowning the flatiron; Carrara
marble; blond brick. It threatened

to plunge off the bridge into the Hollow.
With his pocket knife,

he diced pears into his chiante,
and fed them to me on a spoon.

He wouldn't die for a half a century,
but I missed him already.

Shruti Swamy

Night Garden

I heard the barking at six thirty or seven. It had been a long, hot day, and evening was a relief. I was cooking dinner. I knew Neela's voice well: the bright happy barking that he threw out in greeting, the little yips of pleading for a treat or a good rubdown, and the rare growl, sitting low and distrustful in his throat when the milkman came around—he was a friendly dog. This sound was unlike any of those. It was high and held in it a mineral note of panic. I went over to the kitchen window that looked out onto the yard, where we had a garden. There was a pomegranate tree, an orange tree, and some thick, flowering plants—jasmine and jacaranda—and some I did not know that my husband had planted years before. But I was the one who kept them alive. Neela stood dead center, in the red earth. His tail was taut and his head level with his spine, ears pinned against his skull, so his body arrowed into a straight line, nearly gleaming with a quality of attention. He was not a large dog, black and sweet and foxlike, sometimes shy, with yellow paws and snout. Facing him was a black snake—a cobra—with the head raised, the hood fanned out.

I let out a cry. The cobra had lifted the front of its body at least two feet from the ground. I had never seen one so close, even separated by four strong walls and a pane of glass. I could see her delicate tongue, darting between her black lips. Her eyes were fixed on the dog, and his on hers. Their gaze did not waver. Her body, too, was taut with attention, shiny back gleaming in the low evening light. The sky, I saw now, was red, low and red, and the sun a wavering orange circle in the sky.

Of course my first instinct was to rush out with a broom, screaming, and scare the thing off. But something stopped me. I stood for a full minute at the sink, shaking all over. Then I took a deep breath and phoned my sister.

"There's a cobra outside with Neela."

She exhaled. She was my big sister, and had been subject, lately, to too many of my emergencies. "It's okay. Call Dr. Ramanathan. He knows about snakes. Do you have his phone number?"

I did.

"Are you crying?"

"No."

"It's okay, Vijji."

"I can't—" Then I stopped myself.

"Can't what?" My sister has a voice she could soften or harden depending on circumstance. She kept it soft with me now, like talking to a child. I wiped my face, like a child, with the bottom of my shirt.

"I'll call back," I said.

I went again to the window. The animals were still there, exactly where they had been when I last looked. The dog had stopped barking, and the cobra looked like a stream of poured oil. I dialed Dr. Ramanathan's number.

"Doctor, there's a snake out there with my dog. A cobra. In my yard."

"A cobra is it?" I could see him in his office, his white hair and furred ears. He had a doctor's gruffness, casual in the most serious of circumstances, and had seen both my children through countless fevers, stomach upsets, and broken bones. "Has it bitten?"

"No, they haven't touched each other. They're not even moving. Just staring each other down."

"Don't do anything. Just watch them. Stay inside."

"Nothing? He'll die," I said. "I know it, he'll die."

"If you stay inside the house, he won't die. The snake was trying to come inside the house, and he stopped it. Now he is giving all his attention to the snake. If you break that concentration the snake will kill him, and it will also be very dangerous for you."

"Are you sure?"

"No one must come in until the snake has left. Tell your husband to stay out until the snake is gone."

After I hung up with Dr. Ramanathan, I took a chair and set it by the window, so I could sit while I watched the dog and the snake. It was a strange dance, stranger still because of its soundlessness. The snake would advance, the dog would retreat a few steps. The hair was standing up on the back of his neck, like a cat's, and now his tail pointed straight up. I could see fear in his face, with his eyes narrowed and his teeth bared. The snake in comparison looked almost peaceful. I didn't hear her hiss. The white symbol glowed on her back. Their focus was completely one on the other. I wondered if they were communicating in some way I couldn't hear or understand. Then the dog stood his ground and the snake stopped advancing. She seemed to raise up even higher. Something was too perfect about her movements, which were curving and graceful. Half in love with both, I thought, and it chilled me. Evening came down heavily; the massive red sky darkened into purple.

The phone rang. It was my sister.

"Well?"

"They're still there. They've hardly moved."

"Vijji have you eaten? It's getting late."

I had been in the middle of making a simple dinner for myself and had, of course, forgotten. The rice was sitting half washed in a bowl next to the sink. I didn't feel hungry, less even than usual—I don't like to eat by myself. Instead, I felt hollow, like a clay pot waiting for water. It was pleasant, almost an ache.

"What time is it?"

"Nine thirty, darling—eat something. Shall I come over?"

"No! Dr. Ramanathan says no one can come in or out."

"You phoned Susheel?"

"What's the point?"

"What if he comes home?"

"He's not coming."

"It's his dog too."

"My dog," I said, too loudly. "He's my dog."

Then back to the window. It had grown dark. I hesitated to turn on the light in the house, in case they would startle. Our eyes sharpened as the light faded. There was a bit of light that came in from the street, from the other houses, though it was filtered through the leaves and branches of the fruit trees and the flowers. In it, I could see the eyes of my dog, bright as live coals. There is a depth that dogs' eyes have, which snakes' eyes lack. Snakes' eyes are flat and uncompromising, and reveal no animating intelligence. From there comes the fear?

Now, very quietly, I could hear the snake hissing. The sound had a rough edge to it. Neela advanced. The snake seemed to snap her jaws. I have seen a dead snake, split open on the side of the road. Its blood was red and the muscle looked like meat, swarmed with flies. People said it was a bad omen for me, a bride, to see it then. Imagine the wedding of the Orissa bride, who married the cobra that lived near the anthill, and was blessed by the village. People make jokes about the wedding night, but everyone's marriage is unknowable from the outside. I saw a picture of her in the newspaper, black hair, startled eyes, and I blessed her too—who wouldn't? This same communion, it must have been, two sets of eyes inextricably locked, for hours. The kumkum smeared in her part like blood. The dog was gaining ground. He stood proud and erect, still focused, but doggish now, full of a child's righteousness. His ears pricked up. But then, for no reason I could discern, the weather between them turned, and it was the snake who held them both, immense and swaying, in her infinite power.

Who knows how much time passed. I sat there by the window. The three of us were in a kind of trance. Once, I awoke with my head in my arms; I had fallen asleep right there on the lip of the sink. I blinked once, trying to make sense of the kitchen's dark shapes. It seemed as though I had had a dream of a snake and Neela, engaged in a bloodless, endless battle, and when I looked outside there they were, keeping this long vigil. Their bodies were outlined by moonlight. At this hour, they looked unearthly, gods who had taken the form of animals for cosmic battle. But I could see the fatigue in my dog. You see it with people on their feet for hours, even when they try and hide it, a slump in the shoulders, the loose shoulders of the dead. No different with my dog. He would die, I was sure of it. I pressed this thought against me. The empty house. I would let all the plants die in the yard. I would move.

I find that at night you can look at your life from a great distance, as though you are a child sitting up in a tree, listening to the meaningless chatter of adults. I stood up in the kitchen. It had been years since I stayed up this late. Slowly, infinitely slow, the creatures were inching back, toward the shed at the side of the house, the dog retreating, the snake advancing. Their movements were like the progression of huge clouds that seem to sit still in the sky, and you mark their advancement only against the landscape. I followed them, moving from one window to another. I became very angry with Neela. What arrogance or stupidity had urged him to take on this task? It's easier to be the hero, to leave and let others suffer the consequences. To run barking into the house was all he needed to do, to show me the snake so I could close up our doors.

I stood. The snake hissed up and made a ducking move forward, toward Neela, who snarled, baring his yellow teeth, doing a delicate move with his paws, shuffling back, weaving like a boxer. He let out three high yelps, pure anger, and snapped his jaws, and the snake rose even higher, flaring out her hood, hissing, I could hear it, loudly, like a spray of water. Then she lowered herself. Undulating back and forth on the ground, she slunk away, leaving her belly's imprint in the dirt.

I went outside. The air was clean and cool, thin, as it hadn't been all day, almost as if it had rained. He was tired. He whimpered when he saw me, pricked up his ears, and pressed his wet snout into my hand when I drew close. He was radiant. With his mouth pressed closed between my hands, his eyes looked all over my face, joyful and humble, the way dogs are, filled with gladness. He swayed on his feet with fatigue, then slumped down to his knees in a dead faint, tongue lolling back. His breathing came slow and easy.

    Who had death come for, the dog or me? I lifted the sleeping creature into my arms. He was no heavier than one of my children when they were young, and I took them in my arms to bed. The air was very still outside at this time of night—or morning. Hardly any sounds came from the street, and all the lights were off in the neighboring houses. The air rushed in and out of Neela's body, his lungs and snout. What you have left is what you have. I carried him into the house.

Elise Juska

The English Teacher

It was an unseasonably hot summer day when Katherine's daughter read about the murders. A Friday, in late July. It was the time of year Katherine felt least connected to school—the very heart of summer, when she'd finally managed to stop thinking about the previous semester and wasn't yet in planning mode for fall. It was also the time of year she most appreciated living in New England. Dana reported temperatures were topping one hundred in some places, but in New Hampshire, the cool nights brought relief from the heat.

Katherine looked up from her garden, surveying the pale, sun-bleached sky over the field. She pushed a lock of hair off her brow with one wrist, picked up her cucumber and a handful of tomatoes, and headed for the kitchen door. Inside, she dumped her vegetables on the counter and had just turned on the faucet when Dana called from the living room: "Mom?"

"Yes?" Katherine said, rinsing dirt from her hands.

"Mom!"

Over the rushing water, Katherine heard the note of anxiety in her voice. "What?" she said, shutting off the faucet.

"Did you ever have Nathan Dugan?"

Right away Katherine recognized the name. She prided herself on her memory of her students—would argue she could summon up any one of them given thirty seconds—and with Nathan she doesn't miss a beat. "He was in my 101," Katherine said. She stood, waiting, hands dripping over the sink. "Why?"

"So you knew him?"

"Of course," Katherine said, calmly, but she felt a kernel of worry. "He was my student," she said. "What, Dana?"

Her daughter appeared in the doorway, laptop under one arm, still wearing the rumpled T-shirt and shorts she'd slept in. Her eyes were crusted with dark makeup but her face was alarmed, awake. Dropping to a kitchen chair, she opened the laptop and angled the screen toward Katherine. *Fatal shooting spree in Leeds, NH, mall.* "Oh my God," Katherine breathed. *Suspected shooter NHS grad. At least three dead.*

Katherine sank into a chair. Numbly, she thought: it's another one of those stories. The kind that now seemed to crop up every few months, part of the new American life: the killing of civilians, random but meticulously planned, usually in a nondescript town like this one—not fifteen minutes from their own. The stories were always a combination of the ordinary—the mall, the Friday—and the horrific: the cache of weapons in some lonely apartment, the cell phones ringing in victims' pockets. Dana scrolled down the page. A photo of two stunned-looking teenagers, hugging. A mother clutching her baby, her face such a raw mask of pain that Katherine was indignant it was reported online. And suddenly: Nathan Dugan. *Alleged gunman takes own life*, the caption said. The picture was just his face. It was him, no question, though he looked considerably older—older than the number of years (five? six?) it had been since he was in her class. The buzz cut had grown long, thick, tucked behind both ears; he still wore glasses, but different ones, with metal rims. His skin looked sunken, slightly pitted, his lips a thin straight line. His expression was blank, she thought. It was the thing that looked most the same about him. He'd worn that same look in class.

"Is that him?" Dana asked.

Katherine nodded. "That's him."

"Was he creepy?"

"Creepy," Katherine repeated, testing it. "I wouldn't say creepy, exactly."

Usually, Dana would have rolled her eyes—Katherine was a stickler for language, always looking for the best, the most accurate word—but her daughter had fallen quiet before the pale glow of the screen. "What was he like?"

"He was . . ." Her mind roamed, looking for the right way to describe him. "Formal."

"What does that mean?"

"He was—precise," Katherine said. "He was exact." Other details were returning. She remembered how he sat, hands folded on the desktop, with that same empty expression. He wore button-down shirts tucked into belted jeans, the sharp wings of his shirt collars buttoned all the way to his neck. He'd been ROTC, she recalled, and he walked stiffly, spoke stiffly, as if neither thing came naturally. She remembered his papers—not the content but the look of them, cramped and airless, narrow margins and ten-point fonts. He'd been bigger then, more muscular. He called her Mrs. Daley, even though she always told her students to call her Katherine.

"He wasn't particularly perceptive," Katherine said. "Socially. He was very literal."

"Creepy, you mean."

The air was stagnant and still, the long field behind their house stretching under the hot midday sun. "Something like that."

"Well, if he wasn't then, he is now," Dana said, and she pushed the laptop shut.

They had moved to New Hampshire, the three of them, the summer Dana turned thirteen. The need to move had risen by degrees. For a few years, their quaint Philadelphia row home had been feeling claustrophobic. Jack had a stable roster of freelance clients, which meant his job was mobile; websites could be designed anywhere. They'd both always been charmed by the idea of living in the country, finding an old house to renovate. Katherine had had mixed feelings about leaving the city, her teaching at Penn and column at the *Inquirer*—even now, she sometimes found herself missing it, confronted by an instance of particularly rural narrow-mindedness, a paralyzing snowstorm, or a brazen animal foraging in her yard—but then her mother died, and Dana finished seventh grade. It had seemed the right moment for change.

Katherine was hired to teach two upper-level courses (Journalism, Creative Nonfiction) and one section of English 101 (everybody had to, the dean explained). She didn't mind; she'd always liked the challenge of first-years, liked teaching students for whom everything was new. She prided herself on coaxing even the most passive to care about their writing. *Write what matters,* she told them, *anything else is a waste of time.* And they did—just last semester, Tyler Barrington, a thickly bearded, 250-pound eighteen-year-old and volunteer firefighter, had produced lovely elegies to nature. Greg Cane, who never spoke in class, wrote a moving description of silently building a log cabin with his equally silent dad. Katherine praised and pushed these students; she took pride in the results. On the last day, she was often moved to give speeches. *You've been a special class*—sometimes, she heard her voice nearly break.

She'd always had a harder time expressing herself to Dana, though obviously she was proud of her—member of the National Honor Society, 3.86 GPA, headed to Emerson in the fall. Strong-willed, headstrong—*fearless,* the word. Katherine took pride in this too. Even if, over the past four years, she'd been the one on the receiving end of Dana's willfulness, her surprisingly deep reserves of anger and stubbornness—the sharp outbursts over nothing, refusals to eat anything, repeated threats to go live with her father. At first Katherine hadn't taken her behavior seriously enough. Then came the long shallow cut on the inside of her thigh. *Stop that*, Katherine had snapped, terrified. *Stop it. I forbid it*—in retrospect, the wrong thing to say.

And there was no denying she'd had difficulty expressing herself to Jack. *Emotionally unavailable*—this was one of the more memorable phrases he'd lobbed at her shortly before he left, four years ago, in one of their first last conversations, when he told her he was unfulfilled—*withering*, the word—and Katherine had not helped dispel these accusations by floating above herself, listening with a soothing sort of distance, a faint humming sound in her ears.

Those final arguments, out in the converted barn where Dana wouldn't hear them, had been so ugly, so stunning, they'd left Katherine feeling flayed. *You're so inflexible so controlling you rationalize everything are incapable of seeing things any other*—one subject bled into the next, spilling onto the old barn floor. Katherine had been blindsided. Jack had always been sweet and easygoing (sometimes annoyingly so), but now in the new open air of eleven acres, the muck that had been collecting silently in her seemingly contented husband for eighteen years exploded like a burst pipe. *I need a partner*, he'd said, and Katherine couldn't help but laugh— "partner"? Obviously, he'd been coached. There was another woman. Naturally. A psychologist from Portsmouth. Of course. *She's helped me see how lonely I am*, Jack told her—which, like most things, was a matter of perspective.

With her students, though, Katherine could take comfort in knowing things would never get so messy. She could state her feelings safely, framed by the content of their essays, the language and themes. They were the students and she the teacher—it could go only so far. Even when her marriage was crumbling, with Jack contemplating leaving, and as she drove numbly down the empty back roads to the farmhouse they had been so excited about refurbishing, Katherine had relied on this structure: whatever else was happening at home and with her family, in the classroom she could maintain a certain pose, fervent and energetic, never breaking character, for ninety minutes focused on nothing but the lesson, on the welfare of the bright young people assembled before her. It was one of the pleasures of teaching. You could forget everything else.

Over the course of the afternoon, the Nathan Dugan story grew more terrible and strange, as these stories do. Nathan had been living alone in a one-room apartment near his childhood home in Leeds. In it, police found twenty-two hunting rifles and eight semiautomatic weapons, most of them purchased at a gun shop on Route 18. Nathan had been ROTC during his first two years of college but didn't contract with the Army after his sophomore year (no explanation why, no acknowledgment of the omission—shoddy piece of writing, Katherine thought). Since graduating a year ago, he'd been employed as a stocker at the Walmart in Leeds. There followed a picture of the depressing store and comments from coworkers and a high school classmate. *Kind of a loner*, they agreed (of course). A short, bewildered quote from Nathan's mother Marielle: *He was a good boy.* The death toll rose from three to four. Then the story spun into other larger stories, gun control and the exploitation of the media, which had blithely titled the tragedy Mall Massacre and released audio of shoppers' frantic 911 calls.

Dana spent most of the afternoon on the phone, checking to see if anyone knew anyone who'd been there. Kim Drew's younger brother had been working at the Sbarro in the food court. Laura Mackey, a junior, had been in the Gap and heard the shots. Each story was relayed to Katherine in a rush of breath and feeling; she nodded evenly, numb with relief. The victims' names hadn't yet been released, but by evening it seemed certain no one they knew had been close to harm's way; they would escape the tragedy, Katherine thought, with no personal ties.

When the landline rang around eight, Katherine was just starting on the dishes. She thought it might be one of Dana's friends' mothers—not women she was particularly close to, but they'd been calling all day, a tribe of mothers accounting for their children—but it was Jack's name on the machine. The phone, a black rotary affixed to the kitchen wall, had been one of their favorite details when they bought the farmhouse, a promise of a simpler life; these days, it was merely decoration. Rare that anyone called it, except for the occasional telemarketer, or Jack, if Katherine didn't pick up her cell.

She listened briefly for Dana, the melancholy strains of that Adele song washing down the stairs, and then picked up the receiver with one hand, propping it between chin and shoulder. "Hello."

"Katherine?" He sounded panicked, breathless.

"Jack?" She moved the phone to her hand. "What's wrong?"

"You're home?"

"Obviously, yes. What is it? Are you all right?"

"And Dana's there?"

"She's right upstairs."

Jack blew out a long breath. "I take it you've heard about this goddamn thing."

"Oh." Katherine was relieved, but a little surprised. It was unlike Jack to sound so heated. "Of course," she said. "It happened just down the road." She turned to the counter, facing the pile of unwashed dishes. "It's terrible," she added, her mind roaming for another word, one that would do the thing justice. "It's—unthinkable."

"And Dana knows?"

"She lives on the Internet. How could she not know?"

"Well, no one called me. I tried her cell five minutes ago—"

"She was in the shower," Katherine said. "She's going out."

"Right," Jack said, heaving another breath. "Okay," he said, then he sighed, and his tone grew tender. "So how is she?"

After four years, this was still the place they met and merged, the soft center of their bitterness. When Jack first moved to Boston, and Dana began rebelling, he'd told Katherine their fourteen-year-old was probably acting out to give them a reason to be in contact, united in their worry, hoping that worry might bring them back together. Katherine snapped— *thank your girlfriend for the insight but that's kind of obvious, don't you think?* But if that had been Dana's plan, it had backfired; their resentment toward each other only grew, blame taking root in new and different ways. Maybe, Jack said, Katherine was being too critical. Maybe she wasn't doing enough to comfort Dana, to make Dana feel safe. *Correct me if I'm wrong*, she countered, *but aren't you the one who moved away?*

"She's spooked," Katherine said now, staring out the kitchen window. It was getting dark, true dark, starless—even after five years, it could still catch her off guard, the blackness of nighttime here. "Naturally. She's upset. But okay. They're all okay."

"Thank God."

"They're having a sleepover," she added. "The three of them. At Janie's."

"Oh," Jack said. "Well, that's probably a nice thing."

"Yes."

"Comforting, I mean. Especially tonight."

"Right," Katherine said. She had felt the same way. It was endearing, the girls reverting to their adolescent rituals on a night like this one. In eighth grade, sleepovers had been their Friday night routine: renting movies from the DVD place on Main Street, staying up all night whispering, eating pizza from Mario's, and slathering frosting on saltines. Kim and Janie had been Dana's best friends ever since they moved to New

Hampshire. It was they who sought out Katherine two years ago, showing up together at her office on campus, trading nervous glances as they told her they thought Dana might be *cutting*. (Katherine would never forget the pause she took before the meaning of the word sunk in—foolishly, naively, she'd first thought they meant skipping school.)

"Did you know him?" Jack was saying.

"Who?"

"This kid? Nathan Dugan?"

Faintly, Katherine detected a quick tapping sound. Jack was in front of a screen.

"Because I read that he went to the college—"

"Yes, I know he went to the college, Jack. He was my student."

"Oh," Jack said, and paused. "Jesus, Kate." Silence, a kind of reverence, swelled on the line. The tapping ceased. Katherine could picture just how Jack looked when absorbing news that was sad or shocking: the moment's stillness, then the flexing of his hands, just slightly, as if making sure that, cast in the light of this newly altered world, everything still worked. "What was he like?"

This, she thought, was why English teachers were the first line of questioning when tragedy struck on college campuses; they were the ones who read the students' papers, glimpsed their confused inner lives. Why, shortly after the Virginia Tech shooting, all comp faculty had been required to attend a meeting about identifying red flags in student papers—*indications of extreme hopelessness, violence toward self or others*—and coached on how to respond. *Have you ever thought about killing yourself?* The recommended strategy there, to her surprise, had been to ask directly.

Then Katherine heard another sound on the line, the whir of a garbage disposal, maybe an ice machine. She hated that she noticed, hated that she cared. She knew Jack had had girlfriends (after the inevitable breakup with the Portsmouth woman). At her most spiteful, Dana would refer to spending time with them, though lately she'd been sparing Katherine this information. Maybe it was the specter of college looming, things changing —in just three weeks Dana would be living in Boston, fifteen minutes from Jack.

"Do you?" Jack was saying.

Katherine blinked at the window. She had stopped listening. A sliver of moon hung bright above the field. "Do I what?"

"Remember this kid? Anything off about him?"

Off—this wasn't quite accurate, either. It implied a student who was imbalanced, truly and unambiguously, and Nathan Dugan had not been that. Had he? Katherine squinted into the darkness outside the window, detected a shadowy movement in the garden, a deer or maybe a raccoon.

Katherine had taught in a basement annex of the English building that semester: Room 14C. It was not a good room. Cold in winter, warm in summer. During the coldest months, the radiator had emitted ghostly clanks and bangs. The windows were narrow rectangles at the top of the wall, like holes in an aquarium lid, level with the brick footpath on the quad. Through them she could check the weather—the softly piling snow or pelting rain—and the rush of boots and sneakers, which would thicken and disperse between classes. From Room 14C, Katherine was aware of the world outside, though the world—save for a thin band of light that fell on the footpath in the evenings—was surely unaware of them.

She remembered that class, Nathan Dugan's. After twenty years, each of Katherine's classes remained a distinct imprint in her mind: if not every student in it, then a sense of them, a shape. The configuration of chairs, the size and appearance of the room, and the mood, which was about the distribution of boys and girls, shy students and talkers. From that group, she remembered in particular Ainslie Shay, a sturdy, red-cheeked girl from rural New Hampshire who faintly glowed with self-esteem (which perhaps had been of particular note to Katherine then, her own daughter having retreated into resentment). Hanna Ellison was a hippie and dressed the part—long skirts, dreadlocks, eyebrow ring; she wrote a starkly moving essay about an abortion she'd had at sixteen (Katherine could still remember certain bits—*the menacing gurgle of the aspiration machine*). Connie York had described the heartbreak of her parents selling her childhood home, a Vermont farmhouse—cedar logs, red door, lovely parents hauling wood and heating cocoa; it had been overly sentimental and couldn't possibly have been entirely truthful, but still Katherine had been charmed—jealous maybe—of the unrealistically perfect light in which Connie still viewed her mom and dad.

They were that kind of class: sensitive and serious, eager to share and listen, making it even more regrettable that Nathan Dugan was there. Typically, Katherine liked breaking her classes into groups to generate discussion, but that semester, she'd been forced to adjust. She saw how uneasy Nathan made the others, how they nodded mutely at his bizarre comments (*bizarre*—no, still not right). *You use too many sentence fragments*, he might have said in response to Lauren Hartman's spare, tentative essay about her brother's death in Afghanistan. His comments hadn't been unkind, or deliberately cold. Nathan was simply lacking awareness

—which was far more difficult to address, of course, than a student who was being a jerk and knew it.

So she'd abandoned the discussions, minimizing Nathan's contact with the other students, though the irony was, Nathan seemed largely oblivious to their presence in the room. He'd start talking loudly over someone, prompting Katherine to remind him to raise his hand, and the student to shoot her a sympathetic look—a look that, sometimes, she let herself reciprocate. Ordinarily, if she had a student who was problematic—*challenging*, the word—she felt the others looking at her, trying to connect and empathize with her; this was tempting, but something she tried to avoid. With Nathan Dugan, though, she'd felt the need to acknowledge the difficulty, commend their maturity. She had owed them at least that.

The next morning, Katherine woke at dawn. She put the coffee on, pulled her L. L. Bean boots on over a pair of jeans, and watched the sky grow light. It was a beautiful hour, a private hour. The red barn stood quietly in the distance, *like a postcard*—the kind of lazy cliché she instructed her students to avoid but one she'd used repeatedly with friends from Philadelphia when they first moved here. It still stunned her sometimes, the beauty of this place.

She ate a piece of dry toast and filled a thermos with coffee, then pushed open the back door and started across the yard. The grass was glittering, thick with dew. She noted that an animal had indeed torn into the garden overnight—eaten some of her tomatoes, torn a hole right through her wire fence. As Katherine neared the barn, the bottoms of her jeans grew soaked and heavy. Up close, the old building showed signs of neglect: the shingles loose, the romantic red in dire need of fresh paint. She and Jack had planned on converting it to Katherine's workspace but ended up using it primarily as a storage unit (and short-term battle zone). Katherine hadn't been here since May and, upon entering, was assaulted by the smell—trapped heat, wood, mildew. Something vaguely animal. Dust idled in the shafts of sunlight now beaming through the high windows. As she climbed the ladder to the loft, the trapped heat rose with her. She surveyed her half-hearted studio at the top: chair, desk—an unfinished door propped on two old file cabinets—and the boxes. They covered nearly an entire wall.

Since her first semester teaching, as a graduate assistant, Katherine had saved something: copies of final papers, end-of-semester writing portfolios. It was gratifying to take away a reminder of the hard work done, the progress made. If she rarely looked at them, she still liked knowing that she had them. Now, though, as she surveyed the sagging wall of boxes—soft, pliant, slumped against one another like piles of sleepy children—a wave of exhaustion swept through her. Instead of amassing accomplishments, she'd been mounting evidence.

This wasn't an entirely new feeling. Over the years, Katherine had gotten her share of troubling student papers. Eating disorders, drugs, depression—the personal experience essay, a required part of the 101 curriculum, invited this kind of thing. Usually it was clear the students wanted her to confront them, hand them the number for the counseling center; on occasion, she sat beside them while they made the call. These students knew just what they were revealing. But in other cases—and these, of course, were the far more worrying—they didn't have a clue.

Katherine surveyed the wall, cursing herself for not dating any of the boxes. She grabbed a few off the top and hoisted them onto the floor. Kneeling on the hard wood, she pried open the first box and unearthed a pile of final projects for 101. The papers bore all the trappings of freshmen —floppy plastic folders, bright hand-drawn covers. Some still had price tags affixed, evidence of their commitment. As she picked through the stack, proud, sentimental titles went flashing by. *One Writer's Journey. From Cowardice to Confidence.* A few loose notes fluttered from the pages. *Thank you! This was my favorite college class!!!* Katherine was tempted to pause and revisit these old successes but stayed on task, leaving the first box and moving to the next. This one was older, the cardboard furred at the edges; the pages inside were yellowing and stiff. As she mined through them, dust crawling through her sinuses, her pride began to morph into a kind of sadness. How *aged* it all seemed. All this old energy and excitement, the cheerful covers and personal stories—stories that at the time had felt so urgent and necessary, full of unleashed feeling —relegated to these crumbling boxes, written by eighteen-year-olds who were now adults with children and spouses, probably working in small, dull New Hampshire towns not thirty miles from campus. It might have been better not to keep them at all.

Two hours later, Katherine still hadn't found the box she was looking for. Her fingers were nicked with paper cuts. The loft was stifling—she'd forgotten how the barn collected heat. The windows didn't open, making it an oven on a sunny day. When she and Jack argued, they would be sweating, standing like boxers in a ring. She heard their old fights echoing in the walls, throbbing like old injuries in bones. *You're too critical*, Jack had accused her, in those brief weeks when he'd magically become a person with strong opinions (or else had always had them but never expressed them, which seemed a form of duplicity in itself). *You're too hard on her*, he said. *Being a good mother is more than being a good teacher*—a line so simple-minded it must have been prompted by the Portsmouth woman, who apparently he'd been confiding in about their daughter. Katherine's daughter. *Fuck you*, she spat. The outrage had nearly split her in two.

She swiped the damp back of her neck with one hand. Surveying the remaining boxes, she regretted having started this. It would have been easier, having only her memories to rely on, for memories you could never completely trust—she said as much to her students every semester. *Everybody's reality is not your reality.* She used the dinner party analogy: if four people described the same party, a year later, you'd have four different parties. Memory, experience: these were fundamentally self-oriented. *Every story of what happened is only a version of what happened.* The students got this; they liked it. Their faces would brighten with recognition, probably remembering some dispute with their parents in which they were unfairly maligned. It always worked.

Katherine twisted her hair off her neck, pinching it with a black binder clip. She pulled the lid off the next box, slippery with dust. A roll book perched on top of the pile, the old-fashioned kind she always used, dark blue with raised gold letters. When she opened it, her breath caught—*Nathan Dugan*. Beside his name she'd scribbled ROTC. On the first day of class, Katherine always jotted notes about the students to help remember them; for Nathan, with his buzz cut and stiff shoulders, this would have been enough. She scanned the row of boxes beside his name, a march of slanted check marks. B, B– on his major papers. Absent twice, never late.

Katherine gazed at the old, permanently closed barn window. The sun was bearing in. Her armpits were sweating. She was seized with the urge to abandon this mission, but she took a deep breath and started digging in the next box. And there they all were: that basement classroom, Room 14C. Hanna Ellison's abortion. Connie's tribute to her childhood home. Divorces and dying grandparents, first days of college. (*What would Dana write about?* she wondered—there were so many incidents to choose from, so many unflattering lights in which the mother could be cast—and dismissed the thought.)

As she neared the bottom of the box, she fantasized that by some odd twist of fate Nathan's work hadn't been saved with the rest of them, but there, just as she allowed herself a flicker of hope:

Nathan Dugan
Final Portfolio
Professor Daley
English 101: Section 19

Katherine set the paper on her knees, gently, as if it might detonate if not handled with care. Something about the actuality of the paper was startling: the same boy who would later gun down four people had stuffed—no, probably slid, and carefully—these very pages into his knapsack one spring morning. That same boy had sat in front of his computer at home and typed her name. An old word processor and printer, judging by the square font and green tint. His portfolio had no cover, no clever title or colored binder. She scanned the pages and the look of them was just as she remembered—the narrow margins and boxy, too-small font—but when she turned back to the title page, her heart stopped—

The Hunting Trip.

Her hands turned watery, tingling. A warm flush prickled across her chest.

On a Saturday morning in October my father and I decided to go hunting. We left the house at 6:00 a.m. My mother packed our lunches and stayed behind with the rest of the women—

Katherine noted the casual dismissal of the female gender—subservient, ill-equipped for danger—but reminded herself that sentiments like this were not so unusual here. The bias was something she encountered occasionally in her male students and marked an unfortunate difference from teaching in a city, a perspective so deeply embedded it was difficult to tease out.

We loaded the truck and drove to the woods off of Route 70 near the intersection of Route 70 and Route 18. We wore our camouflage pants and assault vests and face paint and brought our lunches and our hunting gear: which included a compass, a hunting knife, ammo, a muzzleloader, and two AR-15s.

Katherine wiped her damp palms on her jeans. She reminded herself again that these were kids from the country, kids who grew up hunting—certainly this was not the only hunting essay she'd received. Certainly hunting didn't make you dangerous—look at all the locals who converged on Dead River Market on November mornings, filling their thermoses with coffee, dressed in neon jackets, guns stowed in trucks.

But as she kept on reading, rationalizing her way through the pages, there were other things, smaller things, bits of language—always, it was in the language—that she couldn't ignore. The clinical specificity of the ammunition (5.56 mm NATO, .223 Remington) that Nathan had carried into the woods with his father (featureless, except for a brown Mazda B series truck).

And the guns.

I have hunted with many different guns before including: flintlock rifles, caplock rifles, caplock shotguns, pump shotguns, single action revolvers, single shot rifles, lever action rifles, and bolt action rifles. But for hunting the best firearm is the AR-15 semiauto because of the impact at close range. For home invasions or SHTF (Shit Hits The Fan) Scenarios I would use Mossy rifles because they shoot through anything even solid brick so if I had to kill invaders or looters the range and penetration would give me the upper hand.

Katherine's mouth was dry. The rest of the page and the next continued in this vein—a litany of different weapons, different uses, and specifications—pointless tangents as far as the paper was concerned. By the time she reached the last paragraph, her head was pounding. Nathan and his father spotted their kill and, without ceremony, raised their guns. *BANG!* —like an action word in a cartoon. *Right between the eyes.* And that was it. No conclusion made, no insight drawn, no newly forged closeness with his father. There was no meaning here whatsoever, not even an insincere attempt at it—it was as if Nathan wasn't aware meaning was required.

"Mom?"

Katherine jumped, pressing one palm to her chest. "Dana!"

"Whoa," Dana said, raising her eyebrows. "What's with you?"

"You scared me," Katherine said. "You startled me. That's all." She wiped her nose with the back of one wrist, smelled the sour tang of sweat rising from her skin.

"I couldn't find you," Dana said. "What are you doing out here?"

"I didn't realize you were back from Janie's."

"It's almost noon."

On a different day, Katherine might have pointed out that her daughter often stayed at Janie's for hours—sometimes days—but today she didn't care. She was too glad to see her, in her cutoffs and sunglasses, pushing her sleeves to her elbows as she scanned the room.

"God, it's *hot* up here."

"It is."

"Why don't you open these windows?"

"Because these windows don't open," Katherine said. "They've never opened."

"Well, that's helpful," Dana said, propping her glasses on her head. She untwined a black elastic from her wrist, sweeping her hair up into a brisk, emphatic knot. "Seriously, though," she said, taking in the mess of loose papers and dusty boxes. "What are you doing?" She paused on Katherine's lap. "What's that?"

"Nothing." Katherine shook her head. "Paperwork."

Dana's eyes were still fixed on it. "It's by that kid, isn't it?"

"What kid?"

"Mom—seriously?"

Katherine looked at the limp pages on her knees: the march of square green letters, the old staple bleeding rust into the corner—*BANG! Right between the eyes.*

"Holy shit," Dana said, but quietly. "You kept it?"

"You know I keep papers from all my students, Dana."

"What's it about?"

"Nothing."

"Nothing?"

"Nothing significant, I meant," Katherine bristled, but on this point she couldn't blame her. The scrutiny of language was something she understood. She'd perfected it, made a career of it. "It's about a trip," she said. "About an outing with his dad."

"Is it weird?"

"It's—" But she was too warm, too tired and too unnerved, to find the words. "It's nothing out of the ordinary. He wrote about his father, about his family. The kind of thing every freshman writes about."

"Can I read it?"

"I'm not sure that's ethical, Dana."

"What does it matter? He's dead now, right?"

"Well, I think it's a little more complicated than that," Katherine said. She was trying to project authority but was floundering, a headache tightening across her scalp. The truth was, there was no good reason Dana shouldn't read the paper, except that Katherine didn't want to hear what she would say. "Anyway," she groped for a change of subject. "What about you?"

Dana frowned. "What about me what?"

"Your night. Your life. I haven't seen you since yesterday. How was Janie's?"

"It was fine."

"Fine?"

"I don't know," Dana said. Then she expelled a weary sigh, and relented a little. "We watched *Step Up*. Which is an inane movie but had to be done. For nostalgia purposes." She added, "We watched it incessantly freshman year."

"I remember it," Katherine said, and she did. This was back when they had a TV but no reception, when all they could watch were DVDs. It wasn't until Dana's sophomore year that Katherine finally caved on getting cable, an attempt to placate her daughter, fill Jack's absence with other people—people, or something like people—and break the silence as she sat up late grading papers, waiting for Dana to come home.

Katherine looked up from her lap, wiped a finger of sweat from her upper lip. "You'll be careful, right?"

Her daughter looked at her strangely. "Meaning what?"

"Meaning at school. In Boston. I'm asking you to be careful." She paused, pressing her palms to her thighs. "You're leaving in three weeks. Would you just humor me, please?"

"Fine," Dana said. "Fine. Yes. I'll be careful."

"Thank you." Katherine nodded. "It's all I wanted to hear."

The quiet between them was thick with dust and heat. From outside, Katherine could hear the distant sounds of late morning—the tractor at Lyons' down the road, a slow truck rattling by on Route 18. Dana looked down at her hands, squeezed them into fists. Then she said, "I'm going down. It's too hot up here to breathe."

"Agreed," Katherine said, and attempted a smile, but her daughter had already begun to leave. Katherine traced the path of her exit—the creaking ladder, smack of flip-flops, aching slam of the old barn door—and then looked around the room. She surveyed the wreckage. The stacks of browning pages, the dust-filmed boxes. The offending paper still stared up from her knees. Katherine stared back at it—*right between the eyes*—and succumbed to a single shiver. Then she returned the paper to the box. It was unnerving, yes, but also drenched in hindsight. And as Dana said—*he's dead now, right?*

By the middle of August, the world had moved on. The space the Nathan Dugan story had occupied was filled with other things—the New Hampshire primary, Summer Olympics, and all the usual bottom-feeding "news." Celebrity babies, celebrity marriages and divorces. From school, emails had begun trickling in—class rosters, staff meetings, eager students wanting to get a jump on buying books. Usually these things invigorated Katherine, but this year the semester starting was tied unavoidably to Dana leaving. Leaving for college, leaving New Hampshire—Katherine knew it was entirely likely she would not live here again.

On her final morning, a Monday morning, they both rose early. The sun was shining, though the air was sharp with cold. It was a morning deserving of a perfect sky, Katherine thought, a meaningful conversation, but on the two-hour drive to Boston, they barely spoke. Dana was texting with Kim and Janie, Katherine half listening to the garden show on NPR. They snapped at each other as they circled campus, hunting for the right lot, until Dana eventually called Jack for directions. When they pulled up he was waiting, wearing thick urban-looking glasses. He gave Dana a kiss, and he and Katherine greeted each other cordially, and she was struck by the strangeness—how people could be so heated, screaming, and sweating in an old barn, and four years later shake dry hands—and then the three of them unloaded the car. Met the roommate, the roommate's parents, who were married, chatty—*what luck, a corner room!* Katherine started to help Dana unpack, unzipping the zebra-striped duffel bag she'd had since she was twelve, until—*I've got this*. A slight arch to her brow, eagerness in her face. She wanted them to leave. As Katherine hugged her daughter goodbye, her heart thumped with something like panic. Like fear. *I love you, Mom*, Dana said, and Katherine was so caught off guard—by the words, and how easily her daughter said them—that she couldn't speak, and the moment passed, and for the next hour, the highway blurred behind her tears.

When she crossed the state line, Katherine turned into the rest stop: *New Hampshire Welcomes You!* A scattering of picnic tables, ancient candy and soda machines. The sky had grown overcast, undecided. In places, the clouds were flat, gunmetal grey; in others, light struggled through. She opened the windows and parked in a patch of sun. She felt heavy with regret. She pushed down the visor, wiped her wet eyes in the little mirror. She squeezed her fingers in her lap, listening to the swish of cars on the highway behind her. A flat brown hawk circled slowly above the trees. Her ears rang with the quiet—the dull slam of a trunk, alarmed caw of a bird. Finally she set her purse on her lap and dug out her phone—briefly considering calling Dana; no, too soon—and cued up the Internet. It was surprisingly easy to find the address.

The sky over Leeds was dense, bleak, and sunless. Route 18 was monotonous and sparse, edged with long unpopulated stretches of weed-choked fields and brackish woods. Katherine startled when she drove by the gun shop. A small brown building with a sign shaped like a rifle, set in a grassy lot next to a cheap motel that still advertised cable TV.

The house wasn't hard to find—and mustn't have been for the reporters, either. Katherine half expected a TV van to still be there when she pulled up, some trace of the brief, bright media glare. But the house looked unbothered; it looked like nobody had bothered it in years. A dried brown front yard, a porch with a cluster of frayed and broken chairs. A Ford, patchy with rust, sat in the driveway. An American flag the size of a king-sized quilt hung from the porch.

Katherine drew a breath and then stepped out of the car and carefully across the unmowed lawn. A cloud of bugs hovered over a puddle of mud. It was late afternoon and the crickets were chirping, thick and sluggish. The air didn't move. She climbed the sagging porch stairs, but before she could knock the front door snapped open eight inches, secured by a chain.

"What?"

Katherine's first impression of Marielle Dugan was that she wasn't nearly as undone as her home. Through the gap in the doorway, Katherine assembled a pair of denim shorts, a bright white T-shirt, brown canvas sandals. The ribbon of face revealed a sprinkling of freckles, hair a cropped, faded red, a trace of blue eyeliner beneath each lid.

"Mrs. Dugan?"

The woman said nothing. She kept one hand on the door and one on the frame, the dull metal stretched taut between them. It occurred to Katherine, with an odd lack of emphasis, that she might have a gun behind the door.

"My name is Katherine Daley," she said. "I was Nathan's teacher. You must be his mother, Marielle."

"I'm all done talking to reporters."

"Oh, no, I'm not a reporter," Katherine said. "Nathan was my student. In college. He was in my English class—his freshman year."

"I don't remember him taking English."

"Well," she said. "I can assure you he did. I remember him well."

Marielle Dugan paused to absorb this, but her reaction was impossible to gauge; her face, like her son's, was inscrutable, though hers seemed a calculated blankness.

"I just wanted to say how sorry I am," Katherine said.

Marielle waited. The insects buzzed and whined. Katherine's heart thumped in her ears. At home, not twenty minutes away, the August air would be light and sweet, but the heat here was solid and stubborn, soaked into every pore.

"I felt," she went on, taking a breath—she had rehearsed this part—"looking back, there were signs of his troubled nature I might have missed."

Marielle shut the door. Katherine thought she'd offended her, but then the latch tumbled down and the door reopened, two feet wider. Standing in the doorway, Marielle seemed both smaller and more imposing. The living room was dark behind her, except for the low light of a single table lamp. The flowered curtains were drawn. On the mantel sat a picture of Nathan in uniform, looking just as he had that spring of 2008. A gold globed clock, an empty vase. There was no evidence of the father; the house felt indisputably occupied by Marielle alone.

Marielle folded her thin freckled arms, pinning Katherine with a flat gaze. "What do you mean, troubled?"

Katherine's mind churned. She cursed herself for not preparing better answers as she wondered what, to Marielle, *trouble* might imply. Detentions and suspensions—actions with clear repercussions. Her son's strange, insensitive behavior would be impossible to explain to this mother, or maybe any mother.

"Did he disturb your class or something?"

"Well, no." Katherine paused. "Not exactly."

"Because he never got in any trouble in high school."

"No," she said. "I'm sure not."

"He was ROTC. *He was ready to serve his country.*"

"Yes," Katherine said. The heat pressed on her shoulders. She searched for a good word, a fair word, to describe the quality of the language, the tangent about guns—right between the eyes. "I suppose I just felt alarmed about some things he wrote."

"What things?"

She shouldn't have come; she could see that now. She realized she'd expected Marielle to be different—softer, maybe dumber; this was not the person Nathan's essay had conjured up. She wanted to leave, but now she was standing at this woman's door—a mother with a dead son—and needed to offer something more.

"Well, there was mention of multiple guns," she said. "Very specific guns."

The humidity hung heavy, a damp sheet on a clothesline. Marielle's expression was unchanged. Katherine was struck by the sadness in her face—a deep grief in her eyes, and a kind of medicated flatness, the effort behind that thin blue liner.

"Or the way, for example, he described the guns," she continued. "It was notable." She rephrased. "It was—unusual."

"Unusual how?"

"It was—just—" Katherine fumbled. "Just how much he enjoyed them, I guess."

"He always hunted," Marielle said. "Everybody does."

"Yes." Katherine's chest was sweating, her blouse stuck to her skin. She was amazed by her foolishness, her own short-sightedness. Why had she come here? What was she expecting—to be unburdened? Absolved? And for what?

Marielle's gaze shifted over Katherine's shoulder—perhaps taking in the car in the driveway, a Subaru, a college sticker in the window—as Katherine thought of the things she really wanted to know: *Were you worried about him? Do you feel responsible for what happened? What did you miss?*

"Where are you from?" Marielle asked, facing her again.

"Here," Katherine said. She was grateful for the change of subject. "Stafford, that is. But originally, Philadelphia."

"You have kids?" Marielle asked, and Katherine felt something relenting between them, some unexpected kinship offer itself.

"I do."

"Boys?"

"Girl," Katherine said. "A daughter." She added, "She just left for college."

"I guess you probably wouldn't like it if people came asking questions about her," Marielle said.

"No," Katherine replied, startled. "I guess I probably wouldn't." She looked down at the porch, the peeling wood, and felt herself folding inward, her throat tightening. "I'm sorry to have bothered you," she said. "And very sorry for what you're going through and if—I could have done more." Then she turned and stumbled off the porch, past the still, heavy flag. Unlocking the car, she felt eyes on her back, and when she drove away, glancing back once over her shoulder, Marielle's dark silhouette was still watching from the door.

Everybody's reality is not your reality. Heading north on 95, the white sky split open. The landscape began to breathe. The road was fringed with pine trees, the occasional billboard. A seafood restaurant, a liquor store. Signs pointed toward the White Mountains and Maine. A few leaves were already turning—a flame of red, splash of gold.

As she drove, Katherine wondered about her version of that spring semester in 2008. The spring of Nathan Dugan. The spring her marriage ended, the spring her daughter was thirteen—a hard age (in retrospect, perhaps the hardest age) to deal with a move, with a parents' divorce. Maybe Katherine had been distracted that semester. Or cowardly, or crushed. Maybe she had just wanted to be finished with Nathan Dugan, to minimize his presence and focus on the other kids—the more rewarding, more appropriate kids—submit Nathan's strange but solid B average and return him to the world.

As she exited the highway, there was more space, more green. Hayfields sprawled between the charming old farmhouses of Stafford, but when she drove up her own driveway, Katherine felt no relief. She shut off the engine. The house sat dark, the vast yard behind it dissolving into the trees. As she gazed out the window, she remembered a scene: she and Jack and Dana standing there, the night they arrived. It had been a long day, the moving van still packed in the driveway. Jack had gone in search of the local market and come back triumphant, brandishing champagne. Standing at the edge of eleven acres, he had filled three empty soda cans, put his arm around Dana and proposed a toast—*to new beginnings.* Dana had clinked gamely. *Cheers!* Katherine, standing a few feet away, had chuckled. *Isn't that a little cliché?* Now, as the empty field blurred before her, it struck her as a sweet thing to say.

Brian Patrick Heston

The Giants

Giant penguin fossil shows bird was taller than most humans...
The Guardian

They waddle toward an inland sea,
and somewhere beneath its glimmer,

some aquatic mammal (let's call him Bill),
scavenges the rotting hide of a whale.

The penguins screech or honk,
we cannot be sure which. Either way,

they are organized like wolves.
These are penguins after all,

so on land they are ridiculous,
moving in a line like nuns down the aisle

of a cathedral, but there's nothing slapstick
about their bills—long as pikes—

and when the penguins enter water,
they shoot through blue at the speed

of sharks. Only when they are close
can Bill glimpse their blurs out

of the corner of his dim eye. Sand
clouds clarity to murk when he scurries.

You can imagine Bill to be home free
with the sanctuary of his little cave in sight.

It may as well be as far away as the sky.
Bill gets to see the sky only at night,

when the penguins sleep, so moon and stars
are his only reference for what skies are.

Sometimes, as he wades on the surface
in the dark, a thought buzzes his brain.

This fills him with what can only be
described as pleasure. Yet, in this moment,

he simply flees. This strategy has been
failing his kind for twenty thousand years.

That's when the penguins first swam over
from their beaches across the sea to find

his species swarming these waters without
worry. So, one penguin chases as others

hover, and Bill can't see that his path
leads him into a snapping gauntlet.

It is quickly decided, and the water becomes
red cloud. The penguins then pull Bill ashore

to devour. They lean over him like pigs
at a trough, but pigs haven't evolved yet.

Just other mammals that resemble pigs
but are really the ancestors of horses.

Apocalypse Detroit

If you squint toward the smoggy dawn
above the Eight Mile, you'll see dark-suited
ghosts in hats and bonnets wagon-traveling
across Indian country. Vacant Brush Park mansions
catch the wind like flutes. It isn't the music
of Orpheus they make but of Eminem.
They only house zombies now, but zombies
don't exist. The homeless have made a pilgrimage
here to congregate in silence. Even the rats
have left, nothing to eat but asphalt and asbestos.
Like Atlantis, Motown sinks, but there is no sea,
only the Detroit River, filthy as the exhaust
spuming from your grandfather's Cadillac.

Jennifer J. Pruiett-Selby

In Absence

Faces scratched out
from Raphael's paintings like Father
has left, but daddy's not gone

all our faces rubbed free
of dirt and our ancestry

roots like Dutch elms uprooted
whether they carry disease
or just the potential

to break through St. Etienne cathedrals
in Detroit and Gary, Indiana,
when we abandon this place, they'll quake

through the foundation and splint
the domed rafters of stupas

Lalibela churches
carved from single blocks

of stone absorbed by dense flora
in Chernobyl or Poveglia, sanitariums
where we store inmates like Australia

because one day they'll reclaim
Balbec and Babel—ushered to
their pews by Siddhartha

Hemispheres

When of a sudden
time was measured in versus—

in the verses we read
the gods confounded

man's language. We're made
in their image, so we dichotomize:

east vs. west
north vs. south

left vs. right.
But the brain is one

organ, one entity. Sever
the corpus callosum

to end the seizures,
but no more messages

will cross, and communication
between the two will cease.

Be it God vs. man
or god vs. God—

as in the rivalry between
Enki and Enlil at Babel

—we must arm ourselves
with mending tools and press

on. Because They intended
for us to be fertile and fill

up the earth. Though He forgot
to specify *who*, or which two.

So for this, we must ensure
our messengers are bilingual.

Under Pretense of Law

The geese defied migration
this year. They did not fly
south for the winter. No.
Oh, sure, they pretended—we saw

them go overhead, honking.
We watched them, and

They Watched Us.
The geese are up to something.

Just what, we do not know
Yet.

They are conspiring with the ducks.
Of this, we are sure. We have not
seen them together. Nay, we have not
seen them at all, but we are sure the geese

did not fly south for the winter.
We heard them *honk* while we brushed
our teeth. We heard them *honk* while
we showered. While we did our business,

they *honked* then, too. The ducks have
provided alibis, and we all know
ducks *quack*, rather than *honk*. We

are well aware of that fact, thank you.
We only questioned them as a matter of
formality, to cover our bases, and because
that is the law. No, we did not suspect

the ducks. We did not have any reason
to suspect them. They have an unfortunate
association with geese. Due to flight

patterns, and such. They happen to belong
to the same *family*. We don't make arrests
based solely on such relationships. No.
The geese are the prime suspects. We will not
rest until they are apprehended. Because this

is America. Here, the law is The Law.

Reviews

Amelia Gray. *Gutshot.* Farrar, Straus & Giroux.
REVIEW BY KAREN MUNRO

In the title story of Amelia Gray's new short story collection, *Gutshot*, a man is shot in the gut. We don't know why, or under what circumstances—except that the man who shot him sort of regrets doing so. We don't know if the gutshot man deserved it. We don't know his name, or the name of his assailant, or whether they're a pair of cowboys or nurses or chartered accountants.

We follow as the man drives himself to a hospital, where the doctor proves useless, and then to his mother's house, causing her to break out in biblical grief. Within the space of about a page and a half, the man has wandered away to sit beneath an elm tree, where he discovers Jesus sitting on a bough. Spoiler: Jesus isn't much help either.

The story's over within a few hundred words, and we're left not knowing exactly what happened, or how serious it was, or exactly how we should take any of this. Is it a fable? A parable? A dream? It feels like a little bit of each, and it seems to ring some kind of bell in a dusty, closed-off back room of your brain. It feels important and meaningful but not in any way you can pin down or explain.

Welcome to fiction by Amelia Gray.

While "Gutshot" is buried mid-book, it's a great jumping-off point for the collection because it highlights one of the key questions of Gray's work—just how serious are things? Like her gutshot character, the reader searches for some authority figure who can tell us plainly what's happening, what to expect, and what it all means. Again and again, Gray sidesteps the role of author-as-God, leaving the story and its reader to grapple with the implications of the bizarre, intriguing, sometimes hilarious, and often disturbing scenarios she sets up.

In "In the Moment," a man and a woman meet and proceed through the typical stages of courtship. They both put an ice cube in their coffee! They liked the same punk music as teenagers! It's all very sweet and predictable, and it starts out seeming like the kind of light, frothy romantic fiction that fills tables in airport bookstores. But Gray is no Sophie Kinsella. Within a few paragraphs, the couple's growing intimacy has taken a strange turn. Mark conceives a paralyzing fear of losing Emily, telling her: "We are connected in this manner and I am afraid[.]" Emily soothes him, but in no time he's piling up bags of rotting fruit in the kitchen and throwing the phone out in the trash. Next thing you know, they're both jettisoning all their possessions and losing their jobs, and in the story's final scenes, they seem to be dissolving into a kind of claustrophobic, codependent dementia.

Over and over, Gray returns to the idea that love—even pure, untainted, fulfilled, and requited love—is dangerous. In "Fifty Ways to Eat Your Lover," she boils down this notion to its purest, bitterest reduction. "When he buys you a drink," the piece begins, "plunge a knife into his nose and carve out a piece." It progresses from there, eliding the boundary between consummating a relationship and savagely consuming the beloved. And Gray makes it clear that she's not writing about the fury of a woman scorned, or the pain of a failed love affair—the low-hanging fruit, in other words.

The story progresses through all the ups and downs of a life together, through marriage and parenthood and teaching the kids to drive. And then, from there: "When he drives you to the doctor, cut a knot of muscle from his upper thigh with a handsaw" and "When he sits with you for months, chew the tip off his thumb," all the way to "When he says goodbye, eat his heart out." There's no good way out of a love affair, the story acknowledges. Even the best possible course, the one we all consider successful—a long and happy life, togetherness to the end—is still doomed to eventual loss and misery.

So how serious is all this? Well, it's both deadly serious and not so much. Gray's stories are sinister and powerful, and at the same time usually kind of hilarious. In this respect, they shadow some of the masters of the form. A story like "These Are the Fables," in which a hapless couple contemplate their pregnancy in the parking lot of a flaming Dunkin' Donuts, shares at least some DNA with the work of master comic-tragedist George Saunders. In the mordant "Thank You," a pair of women one-up each other's thank-you notes with increasingly lavish reprisals, until the final exchange evokes some of Margaret Atwood's best black feminist humor. And the off-the-wall weirdness of stories like "Christmas House" and "Viscera" is reminiscent of Lydia Davis's terse, emotionally distilled tales.

You have to watch out for Gray's stories—they'll creep up on you. Read them for the delight they offer, and for the anxiety they inspire. Be prepared for anyone and anything to go badly wrong. Know that love is always a double-edged sword. Accept that even if you look up and notice Jesus sitting in the elm tree above your head, you won't get any answers from him. Understand that while it's hopeless to try to make sense of things, that doesn't mean there's no hope. Unless it does. (Sometimes it does.)

James Shea. *The Lost Novel.* Fence Books.

REVIEWED BY JAIME BRUNTON

In "Thinking of Work," the first poem in James Shea's second collection *The Lost Novel*, Shea writes of the work to be done after a storm: "There was much / to do: sun to put up, / clouds to put out, / blue to install." The only response to a storm that is truly effective, the poem's bemused speaker reminds us, is the natural fact of its passing: the return of sun and blue sky, the blowing away of clouds—matters in which we have no say. Instead, we do what we can with what we have, which in this case amounts to patching things up: "(The grass failed. / We ordered new grass")." "Thinking of Work" means thinking of the small ways in which we try to repair, piece together, or clear away the debris. What Shea creates from this "short storm, / short with its feeling" is an opening for thought, for seeing what exceeds the frame of our everyday habits of perception: "Something flew out of / the window and then / the window flew out of the window." *The Lost Novel* doesn't just open a window, it takes out the whole wall.

The openness of these poems is not an apathetic postmodern open-endedness but rather a hopeful grappling in the open air with the fact of uncertainty. The response the poems offer to this fact, then, is not a wholly ironic distance from *meaning* but an earnest striving for *action*. As "City of the One-Sided Sun" explains, "Now, when we're beyond / credulity, can we insist / on knowing what is true / . . . It's the act that matters / . . . The belief in believing, / the faith we have even / in reason, a partial tree." It's in this sense of believing in believing—or believing in spite of the knowledge of inevitable shortcoming—that Shea's work taps into a cultural and aesthetic moment that some have described as "metamodern." Metamodernism, according to its chief theorists, Timotheus Vermeulen and Robin van den Akker[1], is the term that best describes our current after-postmodernism moment, characterized by "oscillat[ion] between a modern enthusiasm and a postmodern irony." And while "postmodern irony is inherently tied to apathy," they argue, "metamodern irony is intrinsically bound to desire." Desire—for knowledge amid confusion, for permanence amid the transitory, for a finished product from the uneven rhythms of an artist's life—is ever present in *The Lost Novel*. When Shea writes in the poem "Plato's Balls," "I heard you say something recently / and I want to make it permanent," we can hear simultaneously the ironic self-consciousness of a voice that recognizes the impossibility of permanence (the speaker jokingly calls himself "a spokesman for the dictionary") and an honest lament for the incurable desire to witness, record, and attempt such permanence.

Vermeulen and van den Akker describe metamodernism as a Kantian "as-if" mentality—that is, the metamodern text, while acknowledging history's lack of telos, nevertheless carries on "as if" historical purpose exists. Echoes of this mentality are heard perhaps most explicitly in "The Phrase You Gave Me," which ends: "My wayward ways are never without purpose. / The purpose is simply not always productive, / a purposeless purposiveness, these days." The repetition of "purpose" in each line underscores the necessity of an end goal, even while the final emphasis is on "purposeless purposiveness"—a phrase owed to Kant's *Critique of Judgment* and describing a necessary quality of the beautiful. The beautiful, according to Kant, must appear to have been made according to a design and affect us *as if* it had a definite purpose, even though it fulfills no predetermined form.

The Lost Novel is beautiful in precisely this way: while resisting appeals to easily identifiable sentiment and narrative legibility, these poems are nevertheless tense, wondrous, and whole. What is "lost" in the lost novel, it seems, is not the story that it sought to tell nor the figures it would memorialize, but rather the novel *form* (or the demands of "form" more generally). When Shea writes in the first two lines of the title poem "I wrote you once for many years. / I called you many names," the speaker may be addressing us as readers, another person, or the lost novel itself. What's important is that the action is in past tense, and that the "you," whether person or work of art, has been "lost" even as the poem itself functions in the here and now to keep the "you" alive, to make permanent the remnants of thought and feeling. The poem closes with the image of a boy staring down a path, ostensibly in the moment just before his death, and the speaker's futile command to the boy (or to himself): "Go back the way you came, / original person." The title poem fails to meet its own comical demand to "Develop character!" Neither does it reach a satisfying denouement that narrative forms typically supply. Rather, it draws our attention to the tragic impossibility of turning back, of locating an origin, and leaves us to answer the difficult question of *what now?*

The Lost Novel urges us to see the power in our ability to ask questions and dwell in uncertainty. It challenges us to "straighten the bend in each [question] mark . . . so that all of those questions were suddenly exclamations, and all of those uncountable questions aligned before a single exclamation mark were an uninterrupted exclamation." It invites us, finally, to join the speaker in "Parable of an Epiphany" who knows, after a life of endless questioning, what he must now do: "I stood up with great pleasure."

1. Vermeulen, Timotheus and Robin van den Akker. "Notes on metamodernism." *Journal of Aesthetics and Culture*. 2 (2010): n. pag. Web. 26 Jan. 2015.

Wendy J. Fox. *The Seven Stages of Anger and Other Stories.* Press 53.
REVIEW BY CATHERINE THOMAS

On the surface, the characters inhabiting the eleven fearless and sharply observed stories in Wendy J. Fox's debut collection, *The Seven Stages of Anger and Other Stories*, appear to have resigned themselves to disappointment. Though drawn with depth and care, they seem powerless to do more than stand by and watch with detached interest as their lives, "go infestive." Even the children in Fox's stories seem to have given up.

In the first lines of the opening story, "Apricots," we're told: "As children growing up in the eastern Washington desert, the dry side of the Cascades, we learned to speak of rain the way we spoke of the dead: with reverence, with longing, without hope of return." Yet more central than hopelessness to each of the stories in this collection, is the longing the narrator of "Apricots" describes. Combing the ground "for green," years after the fire that destroys her marginal but close-knit community, she tells us that, "even a new shoot can withstand ferocious heat."

Fox's writing is deeply attentive to the natural world, and to the physical. Her stories are set out west, in rural eastern Washington, Seattle, and Colorado, and none of the detail of these places is mere scenery. "Fauntleroy," charts the relationship between two college graduates who've settled in Seattle but grew up together in eastern Washington and hold "the same dark scars of perpetual summer forest fires." The female narrator comes to realize: "He and I might have landed in a wet clime, but there are still all kinds of smolder. Think of how a stack of wet rags or a pile of compost might ignite: slowly, and without the drama of a match, of gasoline, of the sky's electricity. It's almost worse."

The physical world is alive in Fox's stories. Sometimes the elements speak truths the characters are unable to voice for themselves. Sometimes objects like cars and houses act as talismans or traps. At other times, they take on human qualities. In "Ten Penny," the narrator's lover M. is a carpenter. She tells us she wants to "lay down in the dark and have him take the cat's claw and pull out all the nails patching me together." It is exactly this minute and ferocious attention to the physical that reveals that Fox's characters are only outwardly passive. No matter how disappointed they may seem, inside they burn with longing. They'd rather have nothing than half a life. As the narrator of "Ten Penny," bereft but resolute, argues, *"No, really, don't believe that line about the glass—*take a full one or nothing at all."

There's a quiet confidence in this debut collection, and a passionate eye both for the subtleties of language and the intricacies of our engagement with the things that can be touched, tasted, and felt. Nowhere is this more apparent that in the title story, "The Seven Stages of Anger," less a story, in fact, than a series of seven prose poems, each of them a beautifully wrought meditation on the themes running throughout the collection.

But it's the final story, "The Eggshells of Everything," which is most alert to the possibility of transcendence. Set, like the opening story, in rural eastern Washington, its voice is breezier and more confident, as is its central character, Mae, who, in the face of painful rejection and disapproval, determines to find comfort in her circumstances. The story, and the collection, concludes with these lines: *"There is no god*, she said back to her teacher in her head, clenching her siblings' fingers through their homemade mittens, *only family.*" Perhaps of all Fox's characters, it is Mae who comes closest to grasping happiness. Whether this signals a new direction in Fox's work remains to be seen. As a person given to irrational bouts of optimism, I hope it does. I am, however, optimistic that readers encountering this or future work by Wendy J. Fox will be well rewarded.

Georgi Gospodinov, translated by Angela Rodel. *The Physics of Sorrow.* Open Letter Press.

REVIEW BY P. E. GARCIA

Georgi Gospodinov's *The Physics of Sorrow*, translated by Angela Rodel, is a genre-bending novel laid over a central theme: the myth of the Minotaur. Gospodinov's work emerges from the postmodern tradition of reflecting on and reinventing myths, a tradition seen in works like Donald Barthelme's *Snow White*, Italo Calvino's *The Nonexistent Knight and the Cloven Viscount*, and Jorge Borges's *Labyrinths*.

In that way—with its ties to postmodern mythologizing and occasionally self-indulgent metafiction—*Physics* feels somewhat dated, as though it might fit more comfortably alongside Calvino than amongst contemporary literature. However, Gospodinov's poignant writing overcomes the cobwebs of postmodern tradition with tremendous success. Unlike many of his predecessors, Gospodinov blends so much of the deeply personal into his work that what might otherwise feel like a novelty of a structure becomes the only means of expressing what it is he aims to explore.

In this novel, Gospodinov explores what lies beneath the surface, a "secret sorrow" that can be accessed only by the narrator's supernatural empathetic ability to enter into the memories and dreams of others:

> Sometimes—at the same time—I am a dinosaur, a fish, a bat, a bird, a single-celled organism swimming in the primordial soup, or the embryo of a mammal, sometimes I'm in a cave, sometimes in a womb, which is basically the same thing—a place protected (against time).

Like the Minotaur lost in the labyrinth, the narrator pulls the reader through the many "side corridors" of memories, blending genres along the way: at points it's fiction, then metafiction, then memoir, then myth. It even includes a series of lists, such as "Things in the Body That Look Like Labyrinths" and "Available Answers to the Question of How Are You." The narrator obsessively tries to a catalog every possible experience in every possible way and his inevitable failure to do so haunts him:

> Why didn't I write down more names? The names of all the places I've been. The names of cities and streets, names of foods and spices, women's names and men's names, the names of trees—a memory of the purple jacaranda in Lisbon, the names of airports and train stations . . .

The reader follows along as best as he or she can as the narrator tries to discover through the darkness the uncertain history of his grandfather, and ultimately, the history of himself.

Gospodinov swings the narrative back and forth through time and space, trying to capture as much as possible, from Ancient Greece, to war-torn Bulgaria, all the way to modern-day Arkansas. Yet the story always returns to the symbol of the Minotaur: on the surface, a much-maligned monster, but in the narrator's view, a creature that has been abused and abandoned, lost in the dark, only to be murdered by those surface-dwellers who can't possibly understand him.

The Minotaur acts as the perfect symbol for Gospodinov's "secret sorrow." One half of him is an animal, an extraordinarily valuable trait to the narrator, who describes animals as having the purest understanding of emotion, unencumbered by language. But the Minotaur still has a human half. While the narrator seems less enamored of humans (at one point, he refers to them as "the animal apocalypse"), he still sees that deep below the Minotaur's animal groans lies the body of a human being—a child, in the narrator's retelling of the myth—who is abandoned. The Minotaur is not completely divorced from humanity, and the narrator stresses that: killing the Minotaur isn't the slaying of a monster; it's a murder.

That human half is also important in tying the allusion back to the narrator's grandfather, who was abandoned as a child and locked in a basement for several months. Gospodinov adds another layer to this by having the narrator lock himself in a basement as he traverses his family history and tries to come to an understanding of his inner, deepest self.

All of this is done in an exploration of sorrow and what Gospodinov calls "the physics of sorrow"—an understanding of its mechanics and quanta, the way that "it can act like a wave and particle at the same time," both there and not there, seen and unseen. The book purposefully becomes a tangle of timelines; characters merge and divide, and their sorrow becomes a unified, animal groan:

> I try to leave space for other versions to happen, cavities in the story, more corridors, voices and rooms, unclosed-off stories, as well as secrets that we will not pry into. . . . And there, where the story's sin was not avoided, hopefully uncertainty was with us.

As one could imagine, that uncertainty can be difficult for a reader to interpret at times. Like many of his postmodern cohorts, Gospodinov's work seems at once original yet familiar—we're at home and yet we're lost, in the deep dark network of stories, trying to find our way to a beginning, or, at the very least, an end.

The often confusing and fragmented nature of the parallel narratives in the novel can be quite taxing on the reader. It demands a high level of attention but for good reason. The novel is a rare work that transcends the conventional story and instead serves as a series of pieces the reader can return to and, upon each return, discover something new.

Contributors

COVER

Breeze Play (detail). Digital print on Japanese paper, collage, 2011. © Trudie Teijink

Born and raised in the Netherlands, artist **Trudie Teijink** finds the subject matter of the 17th century Dutch Vanitas still lifes deeply rooted in her cultural baggage. Formation and decay, the confrontation with the conflict between our everyday activities, and the fleetingness of our existence form a constant undercurrent in her work. For her investigation she uses photographs digitally printed on Japanese paper, traditional prints, and drawings. Teijink earned her BFA at the Amsterdam School of the Arts, the Netherlands, and received her MFA at the University of Nebraska Lincoln, NE. She has exhibited nationally and internationally. Her work is included in the Thomas P. Coleman Collection at the Sheldon Museum of Art, Lincoln, NE, and the Lilli M. Kleven Print Collection, Bemidji State University, MN. Teijink teaches art and studio classes in higher education. Visit www.trudieteijink.com.

PROSE

David Crouse is author of *The Man Back There* (Sarabande Books), winner of the Mary McCarthy Prize in Short Fiction, and *Copy Cats* (U of Georgia P), winner of the Flannery O'Connor Prize in Short Fiction. "I'm Here" is the title story of his recently completed third collection of short fiction.
Kerry Cullen's fiction has been published or is forthcoming in *Indiana Review*, *One Teen Story*, *Monkeybicycle*, and *Hobart*. She is an editorial assistant at Henry Holt and earned her MFA at Columbia University. She lives in New York.
Michael Fessler is an American writer living in Japan. His work has appeared in many journals and anthologies. He has published a volume of haiku (*The Sweet Potato Sutra*) and a textbook (*Design and Discuss*).
Rigoberto González is the author of seventeen books, most recently the poetry chapbook *Our Lady of the Crossword*. He is the recipient of numerous awards including Guggenheim, NEA, and USA Rolón fellowships, and a Lambda Literary Award. He is professor of English at Rutgers-Newark and the recipient of the 2015 Bill Whitehead Award for Lifetime Achievement from the Publishing Triangle.

Elise Juska's novel *The Blessings* was released in 2014 and selected for the Barnes and Noble Discover Great New Writers series. Her short stories have appeared in numerous magazines, including the *Gettysburg Review*, *Missouri Review*, *Hudson Review*, and *Ploughshares*, which awarded her the Alice Hoffman Prize for Fiction. She teaches at the University of the Arts in Philadelphia.

Jay Merill is the author of two short-story collections—*God of the Pigeons* (Salt, 2010) and *Astral Bodies* (Salt, 2007)—and has been nominated for the Frank O'Connor Award and the Edge Hill Prize. Her story "As Birds Fly" won the Salt Short Story Prize and is included in the *Salt Anthology of New Writing 2013*. She is now working on a third collection. Jay has an award from Arts Council England and is writer-in-residence at Women in Publishing. Her recent stories have appeared or are forthcoming in *3:AM Magazine*, *Corium Magazine*, the *Galway Review*, *Ginosko Literary Journal*, the *Prague Revue*, *SmokeLong Quarterly*, and *Wigleaf*, among others.

Achy Obejas, born in Havana, Cuba, has written fiction, poetry, and journalism. She is the author of five books, including three novels: *Days of Awe*, *Memory Mambo*, and *Ruins*. Also a translator, her work includes Spanish-language versions of Junot Díaz's *The Brief Wondrous Life of Oscar Wao* and *This is How You Lose Her* and translations of other contemporary Latin American writers including Rita Indiana, F. G. Haghenbeck, and Wendy Guerra. She is the recipient of the Woodrow Wilson Visiting Fellowship, a team Pulitzer Prize for the series "Gateway to Gridlock" while at the *Chicago Tribune*, a NEA Fellowship in poetry, the Studs Terkel Journalism Award, a Cintas Foundation Fellowship and a 2014 USA Ford Fellowship. She is currently the Distinguished Visiting Writer at Mills College in Oakland, California, where, in 2016, she will begin codirecting Mills's new Low-Residency MFA in Translation.

Shruti Swamy lives and writes in San Francisco's Tenderloin district. Her work has been published in *Black Warrior Review*, *AGNI*, *Kenyon Review Online*, and elsewhere. She has been awarded residencies at the Millay Colony for the Arts and Hedgebrook. She is Kundiman Fiction Fellow. Visit www.shrutiswamy.com.

Laura Elizabeth Woollett lives in Melbourne, Australia. She is the author of a novel, *The Wood of Suicides* (The Permanent Press, 2014), and a short fiction collection, *The Love of a Bad Man* (Scribe Publications, forthcoming 2016). During the last year, she was a semifinalist in the 2015 Script Pipeline TV Writing Competition and was featured as one of the Melbourne Writers Festival's 30 Under 30. Visit www.lauraelizabethwoollett.com.

POETRY

Wendy Barker's sixth collection, *One Blackbird at a Time: The Teaching Poems*, has been chosen for the John Ciardi Prize and was published by BkMk Press in fall 2015. Her fourth chapbook, *From the Moon, Earth is Blue*, was also published in fall 2015 by Wings Press. Her poetry has appeared in numerous journals and anthologies, including *Best American Poetry 2013*. Recipient of NEA and Rockefeller fellowships, she teaches at the University of Texas at San Antonio.

Joseph Bathanti is former Poet Laureate of North Carolina (2012–14). He is the author of eight books of poetry, including *Concertina*, winner of the 2014 Roanoke Chowan Prize, and six books of prose, including, most recently, *The Life of the World to Come* (University of South Carolina, 2014). Bathanti is Professor of Creative Writing at Appalachian State University in Boone, North Carolina.

Karen Craigo is the author of *No More Milk*, forthcoming from Sundress Publications. She is also the nonfiction editor of *Mid-American Review* and the interviews editor of *SmokeLong Quarterly*. She teaches writing in Springfield, Missouri.

Annie Finch's newest books are *Spells: New and Selected Poems* (Wesleyan UP) and *Measure for Measure: An Anthology of Poetic Meter* (Random House). She is the owner of PoetryWitch.com and founder of PoetCraft.org, an online magazine and poets' community.

Todd Fredson is the author of the poetry collection *The Crucifix-Blocks*. He is a doctoral candidate in the Creative Writing and Literature program at the University of Southern California and a 2015–16 Fulbright Fellow to the Ivory Coast. *My country, tonight* and *Think of Lampedusa*, his translations of Ivorian poet Josué Guébo's recent collections, are forthcoming from Achion Books (2016) and the University of Nebraska Press (2017), respectively.

Michael Fulop has previously published poems in *Green Mountains Review*, the *Hopkins Review*, and *Poet Lore*. He lives north of Baltimore with his wife and two children.

Sarah Giragosian is a lecturer in writing and critical inquiry at the University of Albany-SUNY. Her poems have been published in such journals as *Ninth Letter*, *Crazyhorse*, and *Blackbird*, among others. Her book *Queer Fish* won the 2014 American Poetry Journal Book Prize (Dream Horse Press, 2015).

Marilyn Hacker is the author of thirteen books of poems, including *A Stranger's Mirror* (Norton, 2015), *Names* (Norton, 2010), an essay collection, *Unauthorized Voices* (Michigan, 2010), and fifteen collections of translations of French and Francophone poets including Emmanuel Moses, Marie Etienne, Vénus Khoury-Ghata, and Habib Tengour. *DiaspoRenga*, a collaborative book written with the Palestinian-American poet Deema Shehabi, was published by Holland Park Press in 2014. She received the 2009 PEN American award for poetry in translation, and the international Argana Prize for Poetry from the Beit as-Sh'ir/House of Poetry in Morocco in 2011. She lives in Paris.

Julie Henson is the winner of the 2015 *Redivider* Beacon Street Prize in Poetry. Her work has appeared or is forthcoming in *Quarterly West*, *Crab Orchard Review*, *Subtropics*, *Iowa Review*, *CutBank*, *Southern Indiana Review*, and others. She lives in Indianapolis with her cat, Pippa.

Brian Patrick Heston grew up in Philadelphia. His poems have won awards from the Dorothy Sargent Rosenberg Memorial Fund, Robinson Jeffers Tor House Foundation, Lanier Library Association, and *River Styx*. His first book, *If You Find Yourself*, won the Main Street Rag Poetry Book Award. He is also the author of the chapbook *Latchkey Kids*, available from Finishing Line Press. His poetry and fiction have appeared in such publications as *Rosebud, West Branch, North American Review, Harpur Palate, Spoon River Poetry Review, Poet Lore*, and *River Styx*. Presently, he is a PhD candidate in literature and creative writing at Georgia State University.

Lynne Knight has published four full-length poetry collections and four chapbooks, along with a translation, with the author, of Ito Naga's *Je sais*. Her poems have appeared in a number of journals, and her awards include a Lucille Medwick Memorial Award from the Poetry Society of America, an NEA grant, and Rattle Poetry Prize. She lives in Berkeley, California.

Angie Macri is the author of *Underwater Panther*, winner the Cowles Poetry Book Prize at Southeast Missouri State University, and *Fear Nothing of the Future or the Past*, available from Finishing Line Press. Her recent work appears in journals including *Cave Wall, Natural Bridge*, and *New Madrid*. An Arkansas Arts Council fellow, she teaches in Hot Springs.

Paul Martin has published poems in *Boulevard, Commonweal, New Letters, Poet Lore, River Styx, Southern Poetry Review*, and others. His first book, *Closing Distances*, was published by the Backwaters Press. A recent chapbook, *Rooms of the Living*, was cowinner of the Autumn House Press Chapbook Prize, and another, *Floating on the Lehigh*, won the Grayson Books Chapbook Prize.

Bernard Matambo is an Assistant Professor in the creative writing program at Oberlin College. His work has been published in *Witness, Pleiades, AGNI, Cincinnati Review*, the *Journal, Laurel Review*, and *plume poetry* among others. He has received residency fellowships from The Blue Mountain Center and the I-Park Foundation and has served as visiting artist at the Delta Gallery in Harare, Zimbabwe. An excerpt from his novel was awarded the Walter Rumsey Marvin Grant by Ohioana Library, an award given to the most promising writer under 30. He was a 2015 finalist for the African Poetry Prize awarded by Brunel University and is a recent recipient of an international arts education grant from the Minneapolis Foundation to develop a course study of community arts and arts education in Zimbabwe.

Robert Newman is president and director of the National Humanities Center. He has published six books, numerous articles, reviews, and poems, and is completing another book of poems, *Birds and Other Questions*.

Jennifer J. Pruiett-Selby lives with her husband, poet Jason Selby, and five children in rural Iowa. Her work has been published or is forthcoming in *Crab Creek Review, CALYX Journal, Red River Review, Lunch Ticket, Rust+Moth, Ember*, and *Hobart*.

Margaret Randall is a poet, essayist, oral historian, translator, photographer, and social activist. Randall's recent titles include five books of poetry, including, most recently, *About Little Charlie Lindbergh* (Wings, 2014), two books of scholarship, including, most recently, *Haydee Santamaria, Cuban Revolutionary: She Led by Transgression* (Duke UP, 2015). She lives in New Mexico with her partner of twenty-eight years, the painter Barbara Byers, and travels extensively to read, lecture, and teach.

Ron Paul Salutsky, a native of Somerset, Kentucky, is the author of the poetry collection *Romeo Bones* (Steel Toe Books, 2013) and the poetry chapbook *Anti-Ferule* (Toad Press, 2015), translated from the Spanish of Karen Wild Diaz. His poetry, translations, fiction, and scholarship have appeared in *Colorado Review, Tupelo Quarterly, Apalachee Review, Narrative, Juked, Copper Nickel,* and *America Invertida: An Anthology of Younger Uruguayan Poets,* among others. Salutsky lives in Ochlocknee, Georgia, and teaches at Southern Regional Technical College. Visit www.salatusky.com.

Nicholas Samaras is the author of *Hands of the Saddlemaker* and *American Psalm, World Psalm*. He is the poetry editor of the *Adirondack Review*.

Claire Schwartz's poetry has appeared in *Cream City Review, Front Porch Journal, PMS: poemmemoirstory, Tuesday; An Art Project,* and elsewhere. She is a PhD candidate in African American studies, American studies, and women's gender, and sexuality studies at Yale University.

Ephraim Scott Sommers was born in Atascadero, California. A singer and guitar player, Sommers has toured both nationally with his band and internationally as a solo artist. Recent work has appeared or is forthcoming in *Beloit Poetry Journal, Cream City Review, Harpur Palate, TriQuarterly, Verse Daily,* and elsewhere.

Joannie Stangeland is the author of *In Both Hands* and *Into the Rumored Spring*, both published by Ravenna Press, and two chapbooks. Her poems have also appeared in *Superstition Review, Off the Coast, Hubbub, Crab Creek Review,* and other journals and anthologies.

Kira Taylor is an environmental science graduate student at Western Washington University. She has current and forthcoming publications in *Southern Humanities Review, Catamaran Literary Reader,* and *Tule Review*. She lives in Gunnison, Colorado.

Emily Vizzo is a San Diego poet, editor, and educator, whose work has appeared in *FIELD*, the *Journal, North American Review, Blackbird, jubilat,* and the *Normal School*. A San Diego Area Writing Project Fellow, Emily served as assistant managing editor at *Drunken Boat* and volunteers with VIDA, Poetry International, and *Hunger Mountain*. Her essay, "A Personal History of Dirt," was noted in *Best American Essays 2013*, and she was selected for *Best New Poets 2015*. She teaches creative writing at the University of California, San Diego Extension and yoga at the University of San Diego.

REVIEWS

Jaime Brunton is the author, with Russell Eva of *The Future is a Faint Song*, winner of the Dream Horse Press National Chapbook Competition. Her poems have appeared in *Denver Quarterly*, the *Cincinnati Review*, the *Journal*, *Hotel Amerika*, and elsewhere.

P. E. Garcia is the Dead Letter Office editor for the *Offing* and an editorial assistant at the *Rumpus*. Raised in Little Rock, Arkansas, he currently lives in Philadelphia where he is working on his PhD at Temple University.

Karen Munro's work has appeared in *Crazyhorse*, *Glimmer Train*, *Hunger Mountain*, and elsewhere.

Catherine Thomas was born and raised in Wales and now lives in Syracuse, New York. She holds an MA in English from the University of Rochester, and her short stories have appeared in such journals as *Ostrich Review*, *Denver Quarterly*, *Fourteen Hills*, and the *Baltimore Review*.

INFORMATION ON SUBMITTING WORK:

Now accepting electronic submissions. Complete guidelines may be found at http://prairieschooner.unl.edu. All manuscripts should be submitted to the Editor. *Prairie Schooner* does not consider simultaneous submissions. Manuscripts are read during the months of September through April, only.

NEW THIS SPRING

FUCHSIA by Mahtem Shiferraw
winner of the 2015 Sillerman First Book Prize for African Poetry

"*Fuchsia*, culled from robust life and a finely tuned imagination, captures mysteries of the heart and mind alongside everyday rituals. Each poem dares us line by line, and suddenly we're inside the delicate mechanism of a deep song. The magical, raw, bittersweet duende of *Fuchsia* speaks boldly. The personal history and emotional architecture of Ethiopia and Eritrea reside in every portentous poem here. But the stories, each shaped and textured by true feeling, are also ours because they beckon to us." —Yusef Komunyakaa

$15.95, University of Nebraska Press

NEW GENERATION AFRICAN POETS: TATU
a chapbook box set edited by Kwame Dawes & Chris Abani

Each year the African Poetry Book Fund, in collaboration with Akashic Books, seeks to identify the best poetry written by African authors working today. This elegant, limited-edition box set features nine chapbooks: eight volumes of poetry, plus an introduction by editors Kwame Dawes and Chris Abani. The eight African poets included are D.M. Aderibigbe, Gbenga Adesina, Kayombo Chingonyi, Safia Elhillo, Chielozona Eze, Nyachiro Lydia Kasese, Ngwatilo Mawiyo, and Hope Wabuke.

$29.95, Akashic Books

COLLECTED POEMS of Gabriel Okara
edited by Brenda Marie Osbey

Gabriel Okara, a prize-winning author whose literary career spans six decades, is rightly hailed as the elder statesman of Nigerian literature. Including the poet's earliest lyric verse along with poems written in response to Nigeria's war years; literary tributes and elegies; and recent dramatic and narrative poems, this collection is both a treasure for those long in search of a single authoritative edition and a revelation and timely introduction for readers new to the work of one of Africa's most revered poets.

$19.95, University of Nebraska Press

AKASHIC BOOKS **APBF** **UNIVERSITY OF NEBRASKA PRESS**

www.africanpoetrybf.unl.edu

the INDIANOLA REVIEW

Winter 2015 | Issue One

A quarterly print journal featuring the best prose and poetry we can get our hands on.

Reading Period Opens April 15th

Visit our website to learn about our two-week online fiction & poetry workshops!

IndianolaReview.com | @IndianolaReview

———Issue One Available Now———

"*Cimarron Review is one of those treasures among lit magazines—a publication whose commitment to high standards keeps us honest.*"
—*NewPages*'s Reviewer John Palen

Cimarron Review

One of the oldest quarterlies in the nation, *Cimarron Review* publishes work by writers at all stages of their careers, including Pulitzer prize winners, writers appearing in the *Best American* Series and the Pushcart anthologies, and winners of national book contests. Since 1967, *Cimarron* has showcased poetry, fiction, and nonfiction with a wide-ranging aesthetic. Our editors seek the bold and the ruminative, the sensitive and the shocking, but above all they seek imagination and truth-telling, the finest stories, poems, and essays from working writers across the country and around the world.

cimarronreview.com

Oklahoma State University, English Department, 205 Morrill Hall, Stillwater, OK 74078